In His Hands: My Seven—Year Detour Through Cancer

MONICA NELSON

Kaye—
May you always
know
how treasured you are!
Monica I Nelson

ISBN: 1980243256
ISBN-13: 978-1480243255

DEDICATION

This book is dedicated to everyone who walked with me during my detour,
as well as to everyone facing their own.
May your traveling companions be as amazing as mine.

CONTENTS

ACKNOWLEDGMENTS

I've started this story so many times.
It's a story I *want* to tell. And yet, each time, somewhere along the way, I hesitated. I stopped writing and started wondering, "Is it a story *you* want to read?" I wasn't sure. And the notebook got set aside and forgotten. Or remembered with guilt as one more thing I never accomplished.
But, finally, it's finished thanks to many, many good friends and family members who encouraged and prodded me each step of the way.

It would be impossible to list everyone who helped, but there are some names that must be mentioned. First, I need to thank the nurses and oncologists at Dana-Farber Cancer Institute. Without their intervention I might not be here to tell the tale. Carolyn Allard, an amazing editor who read my rough draft and made it so much smoother. Any mistakes were added after and are clearly my own. Anne Mulrain, without whom I would never have found Carolyn (or had homemade whoopee pies). Chuck and Roxanne Anderton, who encouraged me every step of the way. I would have given up years ago if they hadn't kept having me over for dinner to ask how the book was going. Melody Nelson and Wendy Nelson, my mom and sister-in-law, who tag-teamed as secretary, driver, confidant, and caregiver during the detour. Jen Kent, who kept me company throughout my reconstruction. There are so many more, including my coworkers at Lake Street School and my friends at Faith Baptist Church.

The greatest thanks goes to God, the co-author of my life.

1 THE SYNOPSIS

The introduction…

Picture the heroine of this story.

She has brown hair and brown eyes, the former tinged with a bit of yellow, the latter with green. "Moldy hay" and "moss growing in mud" is how she would describe them.

She's quite normal for a heroine – if anyone would dare stretch that word to include her. Average intelligence. Average build. Average height. Well, the word "short" might fit, though she prefers "height deficient."

She always tries to keep both feet on the ground, though rarely succeeds. She smiles often, and loves the rain. She chose a sensible profession, a second-grade teacher. "Paid to sit on the floor and play," she says with a smile.

She shops at Walmart and loves hamburgers and cheesecake. She goes to church every Sunday. She teaches Sunday school and prays before most meals.

She's not super pretty, super talented, super smart, super rich, or even simply super. She's just another human being walking on this earth.

And yet, by God's grace, she became the heroine of this story.

Just another ordinary human, living an ordinary life…

I found out that I had cancer on May 17, 2007. I wasn't really all that surprised – a lump the size of a silver dollar high up on my left breast was a fairly big clue. But the doctors wanted an official diagnosis, so I crawled up onto a hospital bed and took an anesthesia-induced nap while a surgeon punched six core samples from my breast.

Cancer. Aggressive. Invasive. Not hormone driven. Her2nu positive. Chemotherapy. Mastectomy. Radiation. I had to learn a whole new language. My tumor bed was 8.5 x 5.5 x 2.3 centimeters. It was ER-, PR-, Her2Nu+, Node 1. Stage II. The largest tumor was 2.3 centimeters.

But my God is so much bigger than that.

My parents came home to help take care of me and my soon-to-be teenage son, and the treatments began.

The first chemotherapy session wasn't all that bad. My whole family drove out to the cancer institute to meet the doctors and listen to the list of side effects. I sat in a recliner, an IV dripping toxic chemicals into my bloodstream, while my father and son explored the clinic and found supper. Mom sat with me and chatted, and we watched a bit of TV while waiting for the bag to empty. My son held the pillow behind my head the whole drive home. Then I curled up in bed and slept for a couple of days. I never threw up that first time. By the fourth time, I was throwing up in the chair before they could even de-access the port they buried in my chest when my veins proved too picky.

I took my son away for a week of vacation after my first chemo – and my parents came and brought him home when I ended up spending another week in the hospital with a low white blood cell count. That's when my hair started to fall out. When I got home, my dad and I took turns sitting on a stool in the kitchen having our heads shaved.

My mother brought me to most of my appointments during my treatment days. Ultrasounds. Mammograms. MRIs and CT scans. ER visits. And surgeries. She kept careful notes of each visit in her black notebook. "Trip #3," she'd say as we drove into Boston. Then, "Trip #11." "Trip #31." We made a lot of trips together that year.

I had bilateral mastectomies on December 18, 2007, swapping my own recalled breasts for a set of expanders that I had removed a month later to go flat for a year. A year that flew by in a blur of Taxol, Herceptin, radiation, biopsies, heart scans, and wonderful times with students, friends, coworkers, and family.

Then I opted to have reconstruction and had a muscle from my back burrowed over to the front to hold a new set of expanders. Those expanders were swapped out for a set of silicone implants, before the extra fat from my belly was removed, cleaned up, and injected as padding around them. Seven surgeries later, the reconstruction is done, though I'm still waiting to put on the finishing touches and finally have "breasts" again.

It's been a long journey. There have been a lot of ups as well as downs along the way. My job was simply to keep walking. Want to walk beside me for a bit?

2 NOT SURPRISED, AND NEVER ALONE

I kind of expected a cancer diagnosis. I don't know if it was simply a tendency to think the worst, or if it was God's gentle whispering to soften the blow. Probably both. Either way, I really wasn't surprised.

I remember sitting with Mom in a booth at an all-you-can-eat Chinese buffet in Sturbridge. Mom prayed over the food and the upcoming mammogram and then we began to eat, and talk.

I don't remember what we talked about – these days I'm lucky if I can remember to put the milk back in the fridge. But I do remember making an if-I-have-cancer comment.

Mom seemed shocked – as if she hadn't allowed her mind to wander in that direction before. What a phenomenal thought – imagine if we could control the direction in which our minds wander in the wee hours of the night.

My first mammogram had been six years earlier. I'd found a tiny lump in my breast during a spontaneous self-exam. I silently panicked for a couple of weeks then showed it to my mom. Then I went back to the silent panic. If we simply ignore it long enough, maybe it'll go away. That's our unspoken family motto.

But it didn't go away.

Finally, I mentioned it to my doctor and he scheduled my very first mammogram. I was twenty-seven years old.

I once saw a cartoon about how to prepare for a mammogram. Something about lying down on your side by the garage door while your husband opens and closes it. For those who haven't yet experienced one, I can sum up the ordeal in two words: INTENSE AGONY.

4

I'm sure the nurse tried to be kind, patient and gentle; but she really didn't come across that way at all as she planted one hand in the small of my back and shoved me firmly into the machine over and over again. We had to take four different pictures because "he" wasn't happy with it, and wanted a closer look. After a half hour of this, I was ready to go have a talk with "him."

So I prayed.

Prayer is an amazing thing, isn't it? Actually, I guess that's not really the question I mean to be asking. Prayer is simply conversation – with the very Creator of the universe! And isn't *He* amazing? He taught the gecko how to climb a wall. He taught the spider how to spin a web. Just imagine the things He could teach a sentient being – if only pride in our own sentience didn't keep getting in our way.

After the mammogram, I was escorted across the hall into an ultrasound room. This procedure was much less painful – just some warm sticky goo and a cold paddle. There was a lot of silence as the radiologist took pictures of the lump in my breast.

Then the waiting began.

Ask any cancer survivor – or anyone who's had a biopsy and is waiting to see if they've gained admittance into this huge, infamous club – the waiting is the worst. The chemo infusions themselves weren't that bad. Neither were the radiation sessions. And I slept through most of the surgeries. The worst part was the waiting.

Waiting for a diagnosis. Waiting for results of a treatment or gene test. Waiting for my hair to fall out. Waiting for chemo to come or the nausea to pass. Waiting for a nurse to answer a call button or for it to be time to push the button on the morphine pump again. Waiting for my hair to grow back. Or simply sitting in my chair, waiting for the sun to come up so that I won't feel so alone anymore.

Yes. That's the other thing – the aloneness. Getting a cancer diagnosis immediately initiates you into one of the biggest clubs on earth, instantly giving you an intimate connection with perfect strangers. But it also suddenly isolates you – reminding you that you are completely alone, trapped inside your own skin, in a body that has betrayed you.

When you get that diagnosis, you are alone. No matter who is beside you, you are alone. Until, of course, you remember the Creator of the universe who taught geckos to climb and spiders to spin. The very One Who taught cells to multiply, divide, and die. The One Who stretched your skin to cover your bones and heart, and then asked if He could climb in there with you. When you count Him, you are *never* alone.

After that first mammogram and ultrasound, I met with a breast specialist. I didn't have insurance at the time, so I had to pay out of pocket, but everyone insisted that this was something I had to do. He gave me a discounted rate. However, I'm still not sure that I got my money's worth.

The specialist looked at my breast, studied the mammogram and ultrasound reports, considered my age and health history, and then declared the lump a cyst.

"Painful, I know – take Tylenol." He said that there was really no point in removing it because it would simply grow back, though he would take it out "if it would make me feel better."

Of course, because I had no insurance, a "feel-better" operation really wasn't an option for me. So I left his office and, with his full permission and encouragement, learned to ignore the lump.

Once a year at my annual check-up appointment, my doctor would measure it. Now and then we discussed scheduling another mammogram, but I always wrinkled my nose and shook my head, and he never pushed. I no longer did monthly self-exams. I really didn't see the point. I'd already found a lump. Did I really want to rediscover it every month? And if I did find another one, would I have to go through the whole process again?

Hindsight, as everyone who's ever looked back knows, sees much more clearly. I should have done those monthly exams. I should have gotten a second opinion. I should have pushed for a biopsy. I should have had follow-up mammograms.

But I don't beat myself up for not seeing as clearly back then. I was a young single mom balancing a full-time job and a little boy. I didn't have health insurance, and I certainly didn't have another $250 for a second opinion. Plus, I was a trusting and incurable optimist. The doctor said I was fine. So I was fine.

Life was good.

Well, mostly.

Even before cancer, not every day was easy. Some days money got tight. I went on welfare for a couple of years to get through college after my son was born. Some days were lonely. My parents were still in Africa serving God at the missionary boarding school from which I had graduated.

And some days were sad: two broken engagements, one my choice, one not. And the day my grandfather died – time stopped for a moment that day. But that was when God placed a song in my heart.

I was sitting at the kitchen table, gazing out the window and wondering how life can keep going on for some people when it just abruptly stops for others. Then I suddenly felt God's peace. And my heat began to sing.

I grabbed a pen and paper and scribbled quickly to keep up with the words God was giving me. That poem was done on the first draft, no editing required. I sang it over and over again. I still sing it today. I have added a couple of verses over the years – one new one came with my cancer diagnosis. It's my favorite song – the song God placed in my heart.

I think that every life has some deep, deep downs in it. I may look at your life and think that your downs aren't all that bad, or I might feel that they're unbearably horrific. You may do the same with mine. But we shouldn't do that. We shouldn't be comparing. We should simply be surviving. Living. Even enjoying.

It's not the downs that make a life a tragedy. Instead, it's focusing on those downs, and dwelling on them. Missing opportunities to live and laugh because we're too busy complaining – that's the tragedy. There are just as many ups in life. They're simply not as life altering. We dance and laugh through the ups, but we can grow and improve through the downs. We really do need them both. At least until we're done growing. There aren't any downs in Heaven!

The years went by. One summer my doctor moved away, and I found a new primary care physician. Somehow the subject of the lump never came up.

In the summer of 2006, I had laparoscopic surgery for endometriosis. Shortly after that my lump seemed to be growing.

Then one day my next-door neighbor was diagnosed with breast cancer. I remember sitting near her as she cried and talked. She researched different doctors and cancer centers and chose to have her surgery with a Dana Farber surgeon at Brigham and Women's Hospital. I went home and looked at my lump. It was decidedly bigger.

When I began having some other problems, I finally booked an appointment with my primary care doctor. She looked at my lump, made the comment that I should probably have it looked at some time, and then gave me a cream to treat the symptoms. When the cream ran out, the symptoms came back, and she gave me another tube.

Then my gynecologist saw the lump at my annual check-up appointment. Things happened quickly after that. It was only a couple of days later that I found myself sitting with my mom in the booth of a Chinese restaurant waiting to go my second – and last! – mammogram.

The next day, my doctor called to tell me that he wasn't happy with the mammogram results. He called a golfing buddy of his, a general surgeon, who had me come in for a consultation that afternoon. We discussed the symptoms, and then chose a day for surgery. He told me to anticipate cancer. I told him it was in God's hands. We were both right.

OUR GOD
(the song He placed in my heart)

He raises the sun in the morning, and puts it to bed at night.
He wraps me in His kindness, and He is my delight.
 The author of salvation – best book I ever read.
 The Alpha and Omega, the Beginning and the End.
The Creator of cats and children, of smiles and of joy.
He teaches growth through problems. He gave me my little boy.
 His love is never ending. His mercy won't run out.
 His kindness is forever. His laughter – it's a shout.
He is peace. He is forgiveness. He gives a second chance.
He heals and He holds, and He teaches hearts to dance.
 He's a candle in the darkness. The calm eye of the storm.
 A shelter from the heat of day. In winter He is warm.
He turns mustard seeds to bushes, and acorns into oaks.
Imagine what Our God can do with simple, humble folks.
 From hungry snakes to Christmas mice, all gifts are from above.
 He showers us with blessings to remind us of His love.
He causes snow to whisper down so we don't go to school.
He makes the planets spin around. Gravity's His tool.
 He's Lord of all creation. Father, Spirit, Son.
 Beyond all that my mind can hold, He's three but only one.
Nothing breaths without Him, and no one climbs a tree
Without His eye upon them, watching carefully.
 His gaze is on the sparrow. He even names the fleas.
 He counts the gray hairs on my head. He taught the birds and bees.
He is here, but He is everywhere, and He knows everything.
Is it really any wonder that I'm smiling as I sing?
 He's my Liege, He's my Savior, He's the ruler of my life.
 He made me a good mother. He'll make me a good wife.
He is Hope and He is Promise of a glorious shining day
When He'll whisper, "Well done, daughter" as he wipes each tear away.
 He placed the cancer in my breast to teach my heart to trust.
 He helped the surgeons take it out and gave me a new bust.
He is Honor. He is Righteousness. He's all that I hold dear.
And the God Who hung the stars up thrills to have me near.
 My meter isn't good enough. My rhyme can't tell the whole
 Of how He purifies my heart and sanctified my soul.

He once carried a heavy burden. A splintered wooden beam.
He allowed the whips and nails. He hung there just for me.
    For Our God is all powerful. He could have stopped the show.
    But He wanted to continue so we could truly know.
                        Who He is.

3   IN HIS HANDS

On May 17, 2007, I had a core needle biopsy. I had been put under anesthesia because the surgeon had brought in the equipment to do a flash freeze and get an immediate diagnosis. This technique sometimes gives a false positive, but never a false negative. He had decided to remove the whole lump then and there if it wasn't cancer. If it was, he would leave it in order to minimize scarring for the next surgery.

I woke up slowly in the recovery room. My hand instinctively flew to my chest to see if the lump had been removed, but there were too many bandages to tell.

Then my surgeon was by my side. "It's what we thought," he calmly told me. "It's cancer."

As he turned and left, a nurse came over and asked if I was all right. "Yes. I can't feel any pain," I answered, thinking that it was an odd question from a recovery room nurse.

"No," she shook her head and took my hand. "I mean about the news."

I'm not sure that the news had really sunk in yet. Or that I was fully awake. But I was sure that I was okay. "Yes," I told her with a smile. "God's in control."

At my follow-up appointment, my surgeon gave me the specifics. It was infiltrating ductal, which meant that it had already spread within the breast. It was stage II, either T2 or T3, and he didn't feel that a mastectomy would be possible. The lump was so big he didn't think there would be enough skin to seal the incision up again. His recommendation was radiation and chemotherapy to shrink the tumor, followed by surgery to remove what was left of it.

I went home and calmly shared what I knew with my son. He knew that our next-door neighbor had been diagnosed with breast cancer just a couple of months earlier. I mentioned my stage and hers, and talked about my options. Then he stopped me. "What is your stage?" "And what is hers?" He asked both questions very quietly. Then I realized his viewpoint and understood his fears. I was stage II. She had been at an earlier stage. I quickly explained to him that I'd probably been at stage II for a long time and I wouldn't be moving to stage III for even longer – probably not at all with the treatment we were planning. Plus we had an added advantage: We were putting God in control.

Two days later, I met with a medical oncologist in Southbridge. He recommended more testing and scheduled an MRI and a CT scan to determine if the cancer had spread. He also wanted a sentinel lymph node biopsy to be done before I started chemo. When I asked about getting a second opinion at Dana Farber, he agreed to set up the appointment for me, though he was concerned about prolonging the start of my treatments. He was in a hurry.

His secretary called a secretary at Dana Farber, and my cancer care team was created: a medical oncologist, a surgical oncologist, a radiation oncologist, nurses, a nutritionist, a genetic counselor, a social worker, and, of course, God Almighty.

My mom, my best friend, and I took that first drive up to Dana Farber together, and my sister-in-law met us there with my little nephew. I remember standing by a ninth-story window with him, watching the construction trucks in the lot next door during a quiet moment between meeting doctors. It was a bit overwhelming – being the center of attention and learning a whole new lexicon – but I was told that my job was to sit back, relax, and smile. They would take care of the rest. I would be okay. God was in control.

Now, seven years later, I still smile. I'm still okay. And God is definitely still in control. There were ups and downs. There were tears. There were nights I slept by a bucket on the floor, too exhausted to climb back into bed. There were days I just glared at the bald, scarred lady in the mirror. But there was also so much laughter my chest hurt. There were best friends who baked me cheesecake and whoopee pies and a sister-in-law who cut the crusts off my toast.

I would never trade all the blessings I've received in the past seven years for a lifetime cancer free. It just wouldn't be worth it.

You couldn't give me anything on this earth that would be worth trading in for what He's chosen to give me. The good and the bad. The smooth driving and the bumpy roads.

I wholeheartedly believe that God screens our calls. He allows each event that touches our lives, and we may never know all the ones He divinely said no to. We may never know why He said yes to the ones He let through, but we can know that whatever He allows is allowed for a Reason. It's all part of His Plan. He is in control.

I don't always understand. But I trust.

I'm so grateful to be on His mind, that I'm content to rest in His hands.

4   IN THE STATE OF CALIFORNIA

About a month before my diagnosis, my son and I went on vacation to California. It was our dream vacation. Every year, the two of us went off somewhere together. We'd once spent a week on a dude ranch in Texas riding horses and singing cowboy songs around a campfire. We took a five-day cruise to the Western Caribbean where we explored ancient ruins and went inline skating on deck. Another year, we spent a long weekend in a hotel with an arcade and an indoor water park. But this vacation involved my son's lifelong obsession: Legoland!

He'd always been a great fan of Legos, as evidenced by the buckets and boxes full of the little colored bricks down in the basement, and this year we'd decided to book a trip to California.

I had this sinking feeling in the back of my heart that this might be our last vacation as mother and son together. He was going to turn thirteen that summer and was starting to enjoy different things. It wasn't always cool to hang out alone with Mom anymore. So we purposely enjoyed every minute of it. At Legoland, we visited the factory, shopped in the huge store, rode the rides, and toured the miniature world made completely of Legos. Then we went on to Balboa Park, explored the USS *Midway* in the rain, visited Seaport Village and got free ice-cream cones from Ben & Jerry's. We went to the San Diego Zoo, and we swam in the hotel pool. It was a great last vacation.

Well worth getting cancer from.

Because Wesley and I joke that that's where I got my cancer.

You see, a while ago, we bought some fish. They were beautiful black moors – those so-ugly-they're-cute chubby fish with the big bulging eyes. But they kept dying. It turned that out one of them had pop eye disease and it polluted the whole tank. The store then sold me some medicine to put in the water.

Wes read the label and found it absolutely hilarious that the pop eye medicine "has been known to cause cancer in the state of California." We decided that we were quite safe to use it – given that we lived in Massachusetts, basically a continent's width away.

But then, months later, we went to California for vacation and just weeks after we returned home I was diagnosed with cancer. So the running joke is don't go to California after treating your fish for pop eye disease.

Thankfully, it's just a running joke.

The truth is that life isn't that simple, or even that cruel. You don't get cancer just by going to California. In fact, you don't always find the cause of your cancer. It could have been environmental exposure to some hazardous chemical. Perhaps it was simply a malformed gene. I know someone who believes you get it the same way you catch a cold. Maybe it was something I ate or drank. Maybe something given to me by a far off ancestor. Most likely, it was a combination of factors. But I will probably never know.

I will also probably never find out why God allowed me to have cancer. I sincerely believe that He could have prevented it. He could have healed the malformed gene, or stopped the cancer's growth before we even discovered it was there. But in His infinite Wisdom and Grace, He chose to allow it. And – thankfully, joyfully – He has a reason for everything He allows.

I may not find a cause, but I can find a reason. Actually, I've already found a lot of reasons: to grow, to develop trust in the people around me. To learn to place less importance on physical qualities. To find that there really can be contentment in all situations. To become even more patient. To know God better. To discover a brother and a sister who wanted to walk beside me.

My brother and I used to be closer when we were little. However, after moving to Africa when my parents became missionaries, we went to boarding school and didn't have many chances to get together. Although we ate Sunday lunch together every week, we grew apart. By the time we were adults, we were nearly strangers. My grandfather once told me before he died that every night he prayed that my brother and I would grow close again. God chose to answer my grandfather's prayer through my cancer.

After many of the surgeries I recovered at my brother's house, taken care of by his wife and comforted by his children. Because of cancer, I've developed a closer relationship with my brother and discovered a sister.

I may never know why or how I got cancer, but I do know some of the "what for's," and I know it wasn't wasted pain. None of our pains need to be. For we know that all things work together for good for those who are called according to His purposes. Regardless of what we are called to do, or to go through.

So, whatever your pain is today, I'm sorry. I so wish you didn't have to feel it. If I could hold it for you a while, I would. Gladly. Remember that it will turn out good. For now, just know that you're not alone, and look around for a "what for."

Sometimes it's as simple as our loving Creator just wanting to chase us back into His arms.

5 SOMEBODY ELSE'S MISTAKE

At my second mammogram and ultrasound, the radiologist asked me why I hadn't returned six months after the first one as they'd recommended. I informed her that I'd never gotten that recommendation. When I got home that afternoon, I dug out the letter I'd received following my first ultrasound and read through it again. "Noncancerous changes," "not a concern at this time," "recommend follow-up." Then it listed the suggested mammogram schedule – beginning at forty years of age. Somehow, I had fallen through the cracks.

A few people have asked me if I was planning to sue those earlier doctors and specialists for malpractice. They misdiagnosed me. They didn't offer a biopsy to confirm their beliefs. They simply assumed that because I had no family history and I was so young cancer wasn't an option. I believed them because they were the experts. I was paying for their opinion. I didn't know anything about cancer, and I certainly didn't want to.

I didn't know that choosing to ignore the lump would change what could have been a lumpectomy into a no-choice-about-it mastectomy, as well as endanger my life. If we had biopsied that little lump and found out it was cancer, I would still have my breasts. I would still have my original head of hair. I would still have my faith in the medical profession and confidence in my own body.

Of course, there's no way now to know if it was cancer back then. It may simply have been a cyst that over the years developed into cancer. We can't be sure. Now, when I find a lump, I want to be sure. I want them to cut the thing out and study it closely – even when they insist that it's benign.

But would I sue?

No. How could I?

How could I sit here and claim that my whole life is in God's hands and praise Him for being in control, then turn around and sue the doctors for ruining my life with their arrogant choices?

How can I teach that Jesus loves and forgives each of our sins and then demand money from a man who made a mistake? A big mistake with big consequences, yes. But any bigger than my biggest mistakes? Any bigger than what God has forgiven in me? Besides, what is there really to forgive? They were just tools on the Master's bench.

When I first found my lump, I was young. I was a single mother of an eight-year-old child. I was alone, and only employed part-time. I didn't even have health insurance. How would I have paid for any necessary treatments? Even if I went on Medicaid, what quality of treatment would I have received? How would I have handled it all emotionally?

God in His Wisdom had a different plan.

When I was finally diagnosed, I had an insurance plan that covered almost every expense, from rounds of chemo costing tens of thousands each to surgeries and hospital stays without ever a co-pay. I ended my treatment without any debt. Not all cancer patients can say that. I'm sure I wouldn't have been able to say that eight years ago.

Also, eight years ago, I might not have known to go to Dana Farber for my treatments – a center whose only function is to study and eradicate cancer. I knew to go to Dana because my neighbor had led the way.

After her diagnosis, she sat down in shock unable to even look at her test results. Then she began researching. She made a list of the top-five places in the area for cancer research, made appointments to visit them, and made her choice. Two months later, when I received my own diagnosis, I just followed in her footsteps. God had smoothed out the way for me.

My local oncologist's only hesitation with a second opinion at Dana Farber was that I would lose a week of treatment time in the process. He was worried about losing a week, when I'd just lost two months because of a misdiagnosis. But if it weren't for those two months, I wouldn't have had my neighbor's footsteps to follow in, and her diagnosis to soften my own blow. And when my son found out that his mom had cancer, he couldn't have gone to play with the boys next door knowing that their mom had cancer, too.

Also, if I'd been diagnosed with cancer when I first found my lump, there wouldn't have been a cure. My cancer was Er-, Pr-, and Her2nu+. Her2 positive cancers tend to be more aggressive, and traditional hormone and chemo therapies have little effect on them. It was one of the hardest cancers to fight and typically had a poor prognosis, until the development of

Herceptin – a targeted biologic therapy that binds with the Her2 and blocks its effect. Now Her2nu+ cancers are one of the easiest kinds to treat. Herceptin was FDA approved for treatment of early-stage cancer in November 2006, six months before my diagnosis.

My God thinks of everything.

Yes, the doctors made a mistake.

But God was still in control. Even their mistakes fit into God's great plan for my life. So, no, I can't sue them. And, yes, I forgive them.

However, I wouldn't feel comfortable placing my life in their hands again, and I am grateful that that doctor has moved and the breast specialist I saw is no longer practicing. I hope they've grown. I hope they hear my story and learn from our mistakes. I hope they don't make those mistakes again. I also encourage others to do the research, ask the questions, push for the biopsy that will give them reassurance. Be actively and wisely involved in your medical decisions, even while implicitly trusting God. I fell between the medical cracks and my life was changed because of it. But God was controlling my descent.

My God holds the pieces of the puzzle I'm living. He knows what He's doing and He knows what everyone around me is doing. Nothing takes Him by surprise. And nothing can take me out of His will.

His arms.

His hands.

Nothing. Not even cancer. Not even somebody else's mistakes.

6 WHAT ARE SCARS COMPARED WITH STARS?

During my cancer detour, I had fifteen surgeries. The last seven were for reconstruction, four were biopsies, and two were for the port. Then there were the bilateral mastectomies and the removal of the original implants.

The sentinel lymph node biopsy was on June 13, 2007. My surgeon wanted to get a baseline and determine if any cancer had spread to my lymph nodes before we started chemo. The theory behind a sentinel lymph node biopsy is that when breast cancer spreads it first goes through the lymph nodes. If there is no cancer in the first lymph node, there's a high probability that it hasn't spread.

I had been scheduled for surgery at 2:00, but there was a delay in the operating room and I wasn't wheeled in until after 5:30. By that time I had already gone almost twenty-four hours without eating. They quickly set me up with a drip to get some nutrients and fluids back into my system. Then the surgeon injected a dye near the tumor to find the sentinel lymph node before removing three nodes. Because of the long fast and late start, it was a rough recovery. As soon as we got home, I threw up, took a pill, and went to bed.

It took a while for the incision to heal, probably because I started my first round of chemo (Adriamycin and Cytoxan) shortly after the surgery. Cytoxan slows down the healing process. Of course, it also leaves you sore, nauseous, and exhausted. Because of this, I didn't faithfully complete my stretching exercises and I never regained full range of motion in that shoulder.

My surgeon was not very happy about that. However, she was pleased with the pathology report. T3N1. Two of the nodes were enlarged, but all three were soft. There was some cancer in one node and only miniscule amounts of cancer in the others – so small that not too long ago we wouldn't have even been able to find them. It's only today's advanced technology that allowed us to see them. "We can still treat to cure," she told me with confidence.

I was confused when she first told me that. What other kind of treatment was there, if not to cure? As I pondered, it slowly dawned on me how close this call had been. The cancer had already been in the process of sneaking into my lymph nodes when we started chemo. Where was it heading? Where else had it gone?

During one of the scans to see if the cancer had progressed, my surgeon noticed a suspicious spot in my right breast. I went in for an ultrasound, but it was so small the ultrasound technician couldn't even find it.

On July 11, I went in for an MRI-guided needle biopsy.

My two good veins had been used up drawing blood before the surgery, so it took an hour and three people to get a working IV. Then I had to crawl up onto an MRI table. All of the padding had been removed to give the surgeon better access. The nurses carefully tucked a couple of rolled towels in around me to try to make it a bit more comfortable. The table slowly slid into the tube to take some noisy pictures. Then I was slid back out of the tube while the surgeon injected a numbing agent before making a small incision. Then they slid me back into the tube to get another picture and confirm that she'd made the incision in the right spot. This happened over and over again. By the time we were done, I felt like my back and ribs were on fire. I was screaming inside for God's grace, and He provided.

There were three people in the room with me during the surgery: the surgeon and two nurses. One of the nurses was there for the surgeon, getting tools and running errands. The other nurse seemed to be there just for me. She held my hands every time I came out of the tube and talked to me the whole time. "I love your nails." "You're doing fine." "We're almost done." Each time I had to slide back into the tube, she'd place the black panic bulb in my hand and slowly let go. Then she'd be there again as soon as I came back out.

After removing the suspicious spot, the surgeon placed a tiny clip in my right breast to remind us where it had been. Then she stitched me up and sent me home with my sister-in-law to wait for the results. Thankfully, it ended up being benign. My surgeon was very happy when she called with the news, though she warned me that it was not unusual to have a follow-up procedure in six months.

The day after the MRI biopsy, I headed back to Dana Farber to have a port inserted. We got up at 4:30 in the morning to get to the hospital for 6:15.

There were six people having procedures done that morning – five men and myself. At 6:30, a woman came into the waiting room and marched the six of us down a lot of hallways and through a lot of doors while our families waited behind.

We came to a large room with a row of beds against the wall and some temporary curtains propped up between them. The nurse assigned us each a bed and began shouting out instructions. We were all to take off our clothes, put on the hospital johnny and socks folded on the bed, and put all of our belongings into the bag beside the johnny. I pulled my curtain shut, put on the johnny, and then tucked myself into bed to wait. The procedure was scheduled to begin at 8:00.

After I had changed, my sister-in-law and nephew joined me for the wait. It was a long wait for all of us. One of the gentlemen having surgery was irate, complaining the whole time of an allergy to tape and the second- and third-degree burns he'd suffered after his last surgery. Another one was very polite; he'd been through all of this before, several times. He'd had a port for about a year now (and he didn't tie his johnny when he went to the bathroom).

After the phlebotomist got an IV started, the doctor came over to explain what he would be doing. He also showed me the port. It was a purple PowerPort – a heavy-duty one that can handle the contrast dyes for heart and CT scans. The surgeon was going to cut a hole in my chest, then make a tunnel in the fat with his finger and slide the port into place. The cup would sit below my right collar bone, sewn under my skin and poking out like a lollipop pushing against a child's cheek (yes, that's how the surgeon described it). The tube would be attached to the jugular.

Then the surgeon calmly explained that he had to mention the slight chance of going into the wrong vein or artery. I asked how often this had happened. "This week?" was his response. Then he smiled as he informed me that he'd never done that; he just had to say it.

I met with all of the nurses and anesthesiologists who'd be involved with my surgery and I signed the consent forms, then I was wheeled into the operating room. The surgery was done with local anesthesia and a sedative because there were a couple of times when I had to hold my breath. Although I wasn't under general anesthesia, I only remember bits and pieces of it – the foil hat and heated blanket wrapped around my bald head, the box they built up around my face, the nurse who kept peeking in at me. I remember feeling an odd sensation at one point when his tunneling finger touched my bone. Then it was done.

I was suddenly freezing cold and shivering violently. They cleaned me up quickly, gave me another heated blanket, and put me in a wheelchair for the trek back across the bridge to Dana Farber, where we had lunch before searching for a spot to wait for my 3:00 oncology appointment. My new port was left accessed for my chemo infusion later and I felt rather vulnerable walking around with a wire sticking out of my chest, offering direct access to my jugular.

We spent the rest of the day moving from waiting room to waiting room as I met with my nurse practitioner and oncologist, and then headed upstairs for chemo. During the infusion, a volunteer brought us sandwiches and snacks for supper. I also met with a nutritionist who shared a lot of advice about what to eat and what to avoid over the next couple of months.

Finally, everything was done. It was 6:30 p.m. We'd been at Dana Faber for more than twelve hours. That's a long day for a cancer patient, her young nephew, and their caregiver. We trudged back to the car and piled in for the hour-long ride to my brother's house. I carefully held the seat belt out and away from my new port. Every bump in the road seemed to jar it against my collarbone. When we got back to the house, I took an Ativan and crawled thankfully into the bottom bunk.

Within an hour I was throwing up. I spent the rest of the night dozing on the floor curled around a pillow and throwing up into a bucket that my sister-in-law silently emptied every few hours. It was a long night, but I got through it.

The rest of that weekend was spent taking naps and eating small meals. I rested on the couch and felt a bit better each day. When my Neulasta shot came by FedEx, my niece held my hand tightly while my sister-in-law injected it. The chemo nurse had forgotten to order it during my infusion, so the shot came twenty-four hours late, but it would still encourage my bone marrow to grow more white blood cells and keep me out of the hospital.

I rested. And I recovered.

At this point, I was less than a month into my cancer detour and I had already had four surgeries: three biopsies and a port insertion. I had two very noticeable scars, and a large lump where the port was sticking out of my chest. Plus the whole lack of hair thing. Needless to say, I really didn't feel all that attractive.

Now, seven years later, I can't even keep track of all of the scars from surgeries, drains, and IVs. I've even got scars under my scars – odd-shaped bumps and hardened areas of skin where scar tissue has developed around the implants or near incision sites. Twice I've had biopsies of lumps that turned out to be scar tissue and only left a bigger scar behind.

Every now and then, there's a day when I can't look in the mirror without the tears pooling in the corners of my eyes. Days when I think, "This is not what I wanted." "This is not the life I dreamed of as a child." "This is not good." But those days are rare now.

Most days, it's no big deal. Because, in all honesty, what does it really matter? In the grand scheme of things, is anyone really going to care that Monica has a couple of scars? Will spring stop following winter? Will the earth stop spinning on its axis? After all, what are scars compared to stars? To rainbows? To singing birds and purring cats? They're battle scars, and each one has a story behind it. They prove that I'm a fighter, that I'm a survivor. They're now a part of me.

I once got into a discussion with a friend about whether we'd have scars in Heaven. I hope Jesus will have His scars, but I'm not sure if I'll have mine. I won't need them; they're simply reminders of a world gone bad under the influence of sin. In Heaven, sin won't exist. Neither will pain, or tears, or cancer. I won't need a reminder of what He's done because I'll have Him. Some days my longing to be in Heaven is almost overwhelming.

But then I get caught up again in the steady stream of life. I go to work, write a paper, watch a movie, take a walk. I read a book and talk with Abba. I spend time with friends. My life is good. I'm so grateful to be living it, scars and all. Come what will.

Life is good. Heaven is better. God is in control.

7 CHEMO TALES

When I think back on all of the treatments, chemo was the one I was the most afraid of. I'd read just enough about it to be terrified of the side effects: nausea and vomiting, aches and pains, mental confusion and inability to concentrate. What if I lost my ability to multitask, make quick decisions, and be flexible (in other words, to teach)? And then, of course, there was the whole going bald thing.

I had my first chemo on June 21, 2007 – Adriamycin and Cytoxan. I was scheduled to have four rounds of these, one every three weeks. I brought Wesley because I wanted him to see what Dana Farber was like – to see that I wasn't sneaking off to parties or torture sessions, and that I was in good hands.

Mom and Dad came, too.

The four of us crowded into an exam room with my medical oncologist, listening to all of the benefits of the toxic chemicals that I was about to have pumped into my system. Then the doctor left and the nurse practitioner joined us with the list of medicines I'd be taking for the first two days after chemo to help minimize the side effects.

Then she left and a short, high-heeled lady with a mind like an encyclopedia came in and warned us about everything that could possible go wrong. My hair would fall out. I would throw up. My bones and joints would ache for three days. My blood counts would drop and I could get very sick and have to go to the hospital. When she finished, she handed me the consent form. I prayed, and then I signed it. After that we took the elevator up to the infusion floor.

Mom sat with me during the infusion. Looking back, I can honestly say that it really wasn't all that bad. The worst part is the waiting, as my anxious mind explores all of the horrific possibilities and my body tenses up in anticipation of nausea and pain.

My nurse had a lot of trouble accessing a vein for the IV, and we began talking about having a port put in right away. Once the IV was started, a nurse drew some blood to check my levels. When the results came back they ordered my chemo. I swallowed a couple of pills to prevent nausea, then started with a saline drip. One of the pills was Decadron, a steroid with an anti-nausea side effect. It took us about eight infusions to realize that the Decadron might actually have been causing most of my nausea.

I leaned back in my recliner wrapped in a heated blanket, wishing I'd remembered to bring socks and craving a Tropicana Coolatta. Mom ran down to the Dunkin' Donuts on the corner but their Coolatta machine was broken. We passed the time reading magazines, chatting, and flipping through the channels of the little TV above my chair. The nurses offered pillows and heated blankets, and now and then volunteers came by with trays of food to snack on or carts full of books to borrow.

The Cytoxin was a bright yellow and hung in a drip after the saline bag was empty. The Adriamycin was bright red and came in a huge syringe. My nurse draped herself in a thick plastic purple robe and put on huge rubber gloves before she slowly injected it into my IV. This stuff was too toxic to trust to an infusion machine. The whole time she administered it, she was watching my reaction, asking, "Do you feel any stinging or burning?" If it stays safely within my veins it will help shrink my cancer. If any of it slips out of the vein it will create a whole new set of problems.

When the chemo was done, my family piled back into the car and headed home. I don't remember much about the ride home, just that Wesley sat beside me and held my pillow still when I moved, and asked me now and then if I needed anything.

The pillow was a gift from my coworkers. A huge, soft, fluffy pillow tucked into a beautiful pink pillowcase that all of my coworkers had signed. It was covered with the love, thoughts, encouragement, and prayers of my friends. Shortly after my diagnosis, we'd gathered in the cafeteria for a rare group photo. Then, at our end-of-the-school-year staff cookout, my coworkers presented me with a framed copy of the photo, the signed pillowcase, and the promise that they'd all have my back and be by my side each step of the journey. Every now and then I pull that pillow-case out and reread the prayers, poems, verses, and kind words carefully scripted on it in black marker. It's good to feel so loved.

I dozed on that pillow for the next two days, waking up occasionally to complain about the nausea or take my scheduled pills. I never threw up after that first round, but even though I faithfully took all of my anti-nausea pills, I still felt very sick. Eventually we decided that it was the pills themselves that were making me sick. I felt better quickly once I stopped taking them.

After each round of chemo, the nausea was worse and came quicker, but it only lasted for a couple of days. The rest of the time it was a gentle feeling of almost-nausea always in the back of my mind waiting to be triggered. I learned to walk slowly, turn my head gently, and eat frequently. I never went far without a box of animal crackers and a bottle of peach Propel water. I was tired but still firmly in the land of the living. I even went on two vacations that summer.

The first was just a couple of days after my first chemo. Years before my diagnosis, a friend of mine had invited Wes and me to join her and her son for a week of family camp in the Berkshires. The week flew by in a blur of Bible study, archery lessons, treks in the woods, kayaking, high ropes, and good food. At one point I asked Wesley what he thought of it. He was quiet a moment before answering, "I've never felt so close to God." I immediately signed us up for the next family camp.

This year, we decided not to let cancer stop us from going again. It was the perfect place to recuperate: unlimited food, no dishes, lazy days by the lake, awesome entertainment for Wesley, and a palpable sense of God's presence. I spent a lot of time resting in my chair with my feet dangling in the shady lake, just visiting with Abba and enjoying the warmth. My second vacation that summer was a quick getaway to Maine in August with my son and best friend, where we walked and shopped and pretended life was still normal.

On July 1, I snuck out for a follow-up appointment with my surgical oncologist. She told me that she'd seen the results of my last imaging studies and felt that my cancer had already shrunk by a centimeter. The chemo was working.

I quickly grew accustomed to the chemo schedule. First, I'd meet with a nurse to have my blood pressure, weight, and temperature checked. Then I'd head up to the infusion floor to have my port accessed. The nurse would clean the skin over the port, spray it with a cold numbing agent, and then have me count to three and breathe. There would be a quick sharp pain, and then she'd tape the IV line with direct access to my jugular onto the collar of my shirt.

The next step was to head back down to the ninth floor and meet with the nurse practitioner. She would ask about my symptoms and the weather outside, and we would chat for a bit. Then I waited to see my doctor. He would make sure I was healthy enough for another dose before calling down to have the pharmacy fill the chemo order. Then I headed back up to the infusion floor to wait for an empty chair. One day all of the chairs were full, and instead of making me wait any longer, they put me in a private room with a bed. These are usually reserved for the longer infusions.

As soon as a recliner was available, I settled back and relaxed. The nurse would pull the curtains around to create a private spot, and I could read books, watch TV, or chat with friends. I could do pretty much anything except go home. Once I had the port in place, both hands were free. Some days I did cross-word puzzles or knitting. One day I brought all of my teaching manuals and filled out the next week's plan book. Another day I bought a coloring book in the gift shop and colored through my chemo session.

I always got very hungry during an infusion and I did a lot of snacking. However, I learned early on that no matter how hungry I got, I should never eat anything I really liked. It never stayed down long, and my brain made some strong associations. I still get a little queasy when I think about eating at Boston Market, and it took years before I could listen to my son say "Odwalla" without cringing (he still tests this out now and then). I heard one story about a cancer survivor who ran into her oncologist in a shopping mall and threw up as soon as she saw him.

When the infusion was done, the nurse would flush out the port with saline and a bit of heparin. Then she would have me count to three and breathe as she de-accessed it. I'd push down the foot rest, put on my shoes, pack up my bag, and head home.

Nothing to be scared of. And yet, oh so scary.

After each round I would hide for a few days, then get back out there living life for two weeks. Then I'd spend the third week dreading the next round of chemo. It's frustrating because you're finally feeling better. You have no interest in purposely making yourself sick again. Often, the last chemo is the hardest one to go to. The symptoms get stronger each time, and you start brainstorming all kinds of excuses not to go. I got a dead-man-walking feeling. What if this was my last day? What if the cancer killed me? What if the chemo killed me?

But it didn't. Of course it didn't. That wasn't God's plan for me.

After the four rounds of Adriamycin and Cytoxan, I began twelve rounds of Taxol and Herceptin, going in every Thursday afternoon for twelve weeks. Herceptin is a biologic therapy created to target the Her2nu receptors specific to my type of cancer. It's made with mouse DNA and has to be introduced very slowly to prevent my body from fighting it.

My first Taxol and Herceptin combo was on September 13, a couple of weeks after the new school year started. I went in to teach my second-grade class in the morning, and then headed out to Dana Farber at 11:30 when my substitute came in to relieve me. There was a whole new regimen of pills to take with the new chemo combo. I was also given two doses of Benadryl through my IV before the Taxol to help prevent my body from reacting to it. This was when we discovered that Benadryl makes me chatty and prone to wander from my infusion chair to go visiting. I'm usually more of a sit-quietly-in-my-seat kind of person. When my Taxol arrived, my nurse was surprised to have to search the floor for me and walk me my back to my chair.

The morning of my second Taxol infusion, my mother was informed that her brother had passed away. He had been diagnosed with prostate cancer, which had eventually come back and spread to his bones. I was sad that he was gone, though I hadn't known him very well. Two things I always think of when I picture him are the sweet, safe smells of his cigars and the way he visited Grammy in the nursing home every single day. Even when she was harsh to him, or he was busy, or she thought he was her father. He stopped by to see her every single day until she died.

I was also sad because his cancer killed him.

It had been treated. It had gone away. He was a survivor. Then it came back, moved from his prostate to his bones, and killed him. But Mom and I didn't talk about it. We focused on the positives, leaving the negatives right where they belong – in God's fully capable hands.

My third Taxol was the most exciting. According to all of the studies, if you're going to have an allergic reaction to Taxol, you do so on the first or second infusion. So by this time everyone was a bit more relaxed. My Benadryl dosage was cut in half, and my Taxol was administered more quickly. But something felt different.

One moment I was noticing a change in my breathing and wondering if I should tell my nurse. Then all of a sudden I'd lost my breath. I sat up quickly, trying to tell my mom, "I'm having trouble breathing." She glanced at me then reached out and grabbed a nurse who was walking by.

Suddenly everyone was rushing around. My nurse was asking for all kinds of odd-named things and people were responding quickly and calmly. They stopped the Taxol, gave me an oxygen mask, and started up another Benadryl drip. I took slow, shallow breaths and the itchy tingling around my mouth began to fade. Then they paged my doctor. The nurse practitioner, who was on the way to the vet with her injured dog, turned her car around and headed back to check on me. My breathing slowly became steadier, though punctuated by an occasional cough.

I kept coughing the rest of the evening, but there were no other side effects or symptoms. My vitals were good and my lungs sounded clear. They decided to slowly finish the treatment. The next week, I had another round of Taxol with no reaction. However, I began to have difficulties catching my breath throughout the week. When the school nurse listened to my chest, she declared that I had "diminished lung capacity" and called my oncologist for a chat.

After that, we switched to Abraxane for the rest of my treatments. My oncologist assured me that it was just as good as Taxol and it has almost no side effects. There just haven't been the same studies done with it combined with Herceptin as there have on Taxol with Herceptin. It's the Herceptin that matters; they just have to give something with it. I had some doubts, but I enjoyed being able to breathe, so I agreed to the switch. I listened to all of the potential side effects, signed the consent form, and left it in the hands of my oncologist and my Abba.

After my last Abraxane and Herceptin, my mom bought an ice-cream cake from Dairy Queen to celebrate. When she showed it to me (it said "Congratulations, Monica" on the top) she told me that they had written "Happy Birthday, Monica" on the first one. "Ummm, that's not going to work." We laughed as we ate.

I still had forty-two rounds of Herceptin alone to go, but that had no side effects at all. My hair was growing back in and my cancer was shrinking. We had a lot to celebrate. Life was good.

8 I'LL GIVE IT BACK – WITH CURLS

Sometimes God asks for our dreams.

He wants us to place them in His hands. Maybe He knows that what we want isn't what's best for us. Maybe He simply wants to know if we could value Him more than what we value most. Maybe He only wants us to know our own hearts. Whatever His reasons, there are times in life when He asks us to let go of our hopes and dreams and to place them in His hands. But He wants us to do it willingly. We're rarely forced to give.

Sometimes He wants our future. Oftentimes, it's our money. And every now and then it's something that we completely take for granted.

Like hair.

I remember my first visit to Dana Farber, sitting in the examination room surrounded by my loving entourage. My finger twirled a lock of my hair as we each took turns asking the doctor questions, trying to process what was happening to our ordinary lives.

I had long hair at the time. Long and curly. Expensively curly. I paid about $90 each time I got a perm. Of course, I wasn't thinking about perms and curls as I twirled that lock around my finger over and over. I don't remember what I was thinking about.

But I do remember when the oncologist turned to look me in the eye as he said, "All of our chemos will make you lose your hair."

I nodded. My finger kept twirling.

So much had happened that day that nothing was really sinking in.

Later, I pondered what losing my hair would mean. What would I look like without hair? How could I face people without hair? Oddly, what scared me the most was the thought of entering the sanctuary at church.

How could I go to church bald?

I loved my hair and I didn't want to let it go.

Now, looking back, I can see what a small sacrifice it really was. But it was still a sacrifice. It was a struggle to stand in the throne room of my King and slowly pry open each finger to lay my hair by His feet. To let go of what I thought I needed, what I knew I wanted, to depend solely on Him.

But I did. Really, I guess I had no choice. When it comes down to choosing between life or a head of hair, I think everyone would go hat shopping.

I wish all of our decisions could appear that simply. Life, or death.

There are so many things, so many times, when God seems to smile down and gently ask, "And how about this? Would you give me this, too? Do you love me more than this?"

I wish I could say that I pass the test every time. But I don't.

Not too long ago, I received an unexpected check. As I sat pondering and planning all of the new possibilities, I felt God asking me if I'd give the check to Him. "All of it?" I sort of gulped out through a suddenly tight throat. "Yes," He answered, in a friendly, I'm-just-curious kind of way. Not demanding, just wondering.

I debated for days, going back and forth. I wanted to want to give the money to Him. But I didn't want to give it to Him. If I knew someone needed it, I would have signed that check over in a heartbeat. But I needed it, too. I had a son to take care of, a house to save up for. But God is God and is fully capable of getting me a house.

I remember curling up in prayer, coming before Jesus in my mind, hesitant to meet His eyes. Finally, I whispered, "Do you want me to give You the money?" If he ordered me to give it to Him, I'd place it in His hands with no hesitation. But instead, He turned to me and asked, "Do you want to give it to me?"

I can lie to the people around me. And I can lie to myself. But I can't lie to God Almighty. He knows what's in the depths of my heart. Sadly, I shook my head and said, "No."

"Then I don't want it." He sadly answered back. And we sat together side by side. I guess I failed that test. I guess I missed out on an awesome chance to trust God and bring Him great joy. But I grew. And before I got up from my prayer time that night, God had reminded me again that He loves me – even as I am. Win or lose. Trust or doubt. Give or take. Jesus loves me.

All of what we have is simply borrowed, anyway. It really belongs to Him. And sometimes, amazingly, He gives it right back.

My hair began falling out over the Fourth of July weekend while I was in the hospital with a sore throat. When I was discharged, I tucked what hair was still there under a hat, hurried home, and sat on a stool in the kitchen while my dad shaved my head.

I bought a lot of hats, and I received some as gifts. My two favorites were a blue bandana from a friend, and a baseball cap with the caption "No Hair Day" from my mom. I still have the bandana. I've since passed the hat on to a friend who was just beginning her own cancer journey. My insurance company provided a "scalpel prosthesis for chemotherapy induced alopecia" (aka: wig) which I wore once for Halloween.

Soon I became brave enough to "go bald" around the house. And it wasn't so bad going to church without hair. I was the only one who really seemed to care about it. Life really does go on.

By November, my head was covered with a soft fuzz as my hair slowly began to grow back. By February, I was going out in public without a hat. People began calling me Pixie. One friend even made me a beautiful set of sparkly wings. In July, I got my first haircut – a year from the day my father had shaved it off. And by this time, everyone could see the gentle curls toward the ends. It wasn't the fuzzy poodle look I used get the day after a perm. It was real curls. Curls that don't come with a price tag I'll have trouble paying. Curls from my Abba.

It was as if He was whispering down, "Thank you, Child, for trusting me with your hair. Now I'll give it back – with curls."

9 "IT'S NICE TO SEE YOUR HAIR."

I ate lunch with a friend at a diner a couple of years after my diagnosis. We used to meet there for breakfast during my treatments, but hadn't been in a while. The waiter stopped by our table with a smile and said, "Look at you! You've got a full head of hair!" I just smiled back. That wasn't the first comment I'd gotten about my hair.

I started my harshest chemo treatments over the summer of 2007. By the time school started up again, I was completely bald and very nervous about how my students and coworkers would react. I tried wearing a wig. I actually did wear it for the whole drive in to work that first day back, but then I pulled it off and wore my favorite blue bandana instead. The wig was just too hot and itchy, and it's quite hard to concentrate on teaching double digit addition when you're wondering if your hair is on crooked.

My new students didn't really seem to notice that I was any different than the other teachers in the building, but my previous students all knew that something was up. One boy stopped by my room and started crying. I told him I was fine and gave him a huge hug. Every time he walked by my room for the rest of the year, he knocked on my window, smiled, and waved to me.

Another former student, a rather vocal young lady, walked right up to me to ask if the rumors were true. "Miss Nelson," she asked. "What do you have under your hat?"

"My head." I answered seriously.

"Phew!" she almost shouted, suddenly looking very relieved. "They said you were bald." This was the same child who, shortly after my diagnosis, had come flying into the classroom, thrown her arms around me, and begged me, "Please don't die!" I told her I wouldn't. That I would be okay. She let go of me, smiled, and went on with her work.

The neat thing about children is that if you tell them something is normal, they accept it. Throughout all of my treatments, I could be myself in my classroom.

It was a little harder everywhere else. I was always wondering what people were thinking when they saw my head. What they were saying when I left the room. For me, everything seemed to revolve around my baldness.

One evening the church youth group had a gathering. The theme was crazy hair night. I decided to stop by and, because of the theme, I went hatless. One of my friends saw me walk in the door and shouted out, "Monica! It's nice to see you're here!" I momentarily misinterpreted it as "It's nice to see your hair."

My first chemo was on June 23. The next week, my son and I headed to Lakeside Christian Camp for two weeks of vacation. On the way, we wondered how my hair would fall out. I'd read stories of women who'd lost their hair in odd ways: one had clumps blowing out the sunroof when she went for a car ride. When I told that story to a friend, she suddenly became very interested in going tubing together at camp. She had visions of me getting on the tube with a full head of hair and crawling off it bald. But it didn't happen that way.

About a week and a half into our vacation, I ended up checking into the Berkshire Medical Center with an extremely low white blood cell count. I had absolutely no immunities to anything and I got a couple of days of free room and board in a private room.

After watching TV, reading a book, writing, and watching some more TV, I got quite bored and ran my hands through my hair in a quick gesture of frustration. That's when I noticed my hair had started to fall out. There were probably ten to twenty hairs stuck between my fingers. I shook them off and ran my fingers through again. There were a few more loose hairs. No huge clumps, just a couple of strands. But over and over again. Finally, I leaned over the edge of the bed and looked down. There was a huge pile of hair on the floor. I jumped out of bed, grabbed my IV drip, and headed to the bathroom mirror to see what I looked like bald. Amazingly, I didn't look any different at all. There had to have been over a thousand hairs on the floor, but I still had a full mop of hair on my head.

This became my favorite pastime over the next couple of days. Just running my fingers through my hair, guessing how many hairs were in my hand, and shaking them onto the floor. The cleaning lady audibly gasped the first time she stopped by. Then she swept it up and began coming by twice a day.

One day my doctor stopped in for a chat. We talked about card games and internal organs. He showed me how to feel my colon and shared some other useless skills. Then, on his way out, he said, "You know, if it were me in that hospital bed, I'd be sitting there pulling my hair out." I just smiled and nodded at him as he left the room, running my fingers gently through my hair.

By the time I was allowed to leave, there was a noticeable thinning. I have no idea how many hairs I'd shaken onto the floor; I lost count that first day. But God knows. He had numbered each one of those hairs. And He's numbered all the ones that grew back. All the ones I have right now.

Because it did grow back. One morning, in the shower, I caught sight of something large and black out of the corner of my eye. I jumped back thinking that some huge bug had snuck into the shower with me only to discover that it was my own hair, lengthened by the weight of the water. This was the first time I'd been able to see it without a mirror since I'd shaved my head. Another time, I was leaning down to talk to a first grader in bus line. My hair fell forward and she ran her fingers through it. "You have pretty hair," she smiled up at me. Not too long after that, it was finally long enough to put in a ponytail. Then it was long enough to put in a pony tail and braid. Soon after one of my coworkers told me that it was longer than she'd ever seen it. Shortly after that, I donated a foot of it to Locks for Love. Now, I'm growing it out again. A coworker commented just the other day about how long it's getting again, and how curly the ends are.

Growing it longer is my way of taking back a little of what the cancer stole. A way to make things okay again. To chase away a bit of the pain left over from losing it in the first place, and a bit of the fear of losing it again. Maybe even to pretend that I have some control over some part of my life.

Donating it is my way of triumphing over cancer. Of sharing my hope with someone who's about to really need it.

I think my Abba likes that idea. And I think He's okay with me clinging to my hair a bit now and then. He knows I'm clinging even more tightly to Him. He knows I'll let it go whenever He asks.

One day a few years ago I was standing on the front steps of the school after bringing my students out to their buses. One of the bus drivers got out of her bus and ran up to me. "I've just been diagnosed with cancer," she told me. "But this," she reached out and grasped a lock of my long hair, "this gives me hope."

God doesn't always ask us to let go. Sometimes He gives, and lets us hold loosely, knowing we're willing to let go when the moment comes. Sometimes

He lets us choose and loves us despite our choice. Maybe He's smiling down at me right now whispering, "Yes. It *is* nice to see your hair."

10 ONE LUMP, OR TWO?

Some decisions just shouldn't have to be made.

I remember the day of my diagnosis, trying to absorb and process all the new information. I had cancer. My breast needed to be removed before the cancer spread and I died. We weren't talking stages yet, I hadn't heard about positive and negative receptors yet. But I was already trying to decide – one lump or two?

There were so many factors to consider. Would removing the second breast keep the cancer from coming back? Would it make it easier for a plastic surgeon to create matching breasts later? Would I want that other breast if I ever ended up having another child? Would I ever be willing to have another child with the risk of the cancer coming back?

Two days after the surgery I'd firmly decided that I wanted to have a single mastectomy with reconstruction. This was a body that God had created and given me to steward and I had an obligation to take care of it. I wanted to get the cancer out in whatever way would do the least damage and leave me feeling the least miserable.

After my first meeting with my plastic surgeon, I was back on the fence. If I had one breast removed, she could use my stomach muscles to create a small breast. If I remove both breasts, she could put in expanders and stretch the skin before radiation. Then after radiation, she would put in silicone implants. Having two breasts removed could make later symmetry easier. If I opted for a single mastectomy and then ever gained or lost a lot of weight, the natural breast would change in size while the reconstructed one stayed the same. Also, with age and time the natural breast would begin to sag while the reconstructed one would stay where it was placed.

Because I'd probably end up having another biopsy on the right breast in the future anyway, why not remove the risk of cancer now? Cosmetically, bilateral mastectomies seemed the wiser choice.

When I met with my surgical oncologist, she carefully explained that having bilateral mastectomies would have no impact on my survival rate. My chance of developing cancer in my right breast is only 1% more per year than everyone else out there. And my survival rate is based solely on the diagnosed cancer in my left breast. In my situation, there was no medical benefit to removing the right breast. However, there was that clip placed there during the MRI-guided biopsy, along with the possible need to biopsy it again in six months. Simply removing that breast would give peace of mind.

Apparently, the younger a breast cancer patient is, the more likely she will be to choose bilateral mastectomies. The desire to avoid risk is higher than the fear of surgery. Older patients are usually more willing to take the risk of a repeat cancer over the discomfort of another surgery.

In the end, the piece of information that helped the most was a chance comment. I don't even remember who said it, but as soon as I heard it my decision was made. It turns out that after a mastectomy, mammograms are unnecessary. I decided to go with two.

11 GOING FLAT

I'm no Barbie Doll. I never was and I never will be. It took a tango with cancer for me to realize that that's okay.

By the time I was diagnosed, the choice between a lumpectomy or a mastectomy had been taken away from me. The lump was large, and too much breast tissue was involved. Plus, there were some cancer cells in the lymph nodes. I had to have a mastectomy. I had to remove my breast.

My doctors were all quick to reassure me that today there are many, many options available for reconstruction, and I was sent to talk with a plastic surgeon. Her first thought, which probably should not have come out of her mouth, was, "Because you're so small, if I were you I'd simply remove them both and go flat." She may have seen the look of horror on my face, as she added quietly, "Maybe have some nipples tattooed—" Her voice trailed away and we sat in silence for a bit.

Other options included using my stomach or my back muscles to create a small left breast and maybe adding silicone implants, or using expanders to stretch the muscle before adding silicone implants. The down-side of expanders was that they could not be in place during the radiation that I would start two months after the surgery. Also, after radiation, the skin would no longer be able to stretch. We'd have to use rapid expansion to reach the right size before the radiation treatments began. Using my back or my stomach muscles also had some downsides such as the added healing time, the extra scars, and the minor complications that come along with missing muscles.

I've never been very good at making up my mind about anything, and this decision just felt so huge! It took a lot of prayer to make my choice, and I'm glad I made the choice I did, even though things did not work out at all as we expected.

I chose rapid expansion.

The first step was to get the insurance company to agree to it. My plastic surgeon wanted to use a "regenerative tissue matrix" to create pockets to hold the expander. She tried explaining what this was, but I decided to stop listening after the word "cadaver." My insurance company deemed this an experimental procedure and refused to cover it. At this point, my surgeon's advice was to find a new insurance company. Her second suggestion was to set up a payment plan for me to pay the several thousand dollars myself. However, as a single mother on a teaching salary, breasts just don't make the shopping list. Neither of these were options for me. Finally, the surgeon decided that she could do the procedure without the regenerative tissue matrix.

At this point, my insurance company decided that the plastic surgeon herself would not be covered because she was out of network. My surgery was already set and the mastectomies could not be postponed. My surgical oncologist made some phone calls and the insurance company agreed to make an exception.

We did the eight-hour procedure on December 18, 2007. My surgical oncologist began on the left side, opening the breast and scooping out all of the breast tissue, removing the lump and the nipple while saving as much skin as possible. Then, when she moved to the second side, the plastic surgeon stepped up and began rebuilding the first breast. She slipped in expanders and put in two hundred ccs of saline.

Because I was having bilateral mastectomies, my insurance company paid for two nights in the hospital. The day in between those two nights was a fuzzy, painful blur. I listened to music and clutched my morphine drip button. The first night my fever spiked to 102. The second night it went up to 101. There was some debate about keeping me for a third night, but they decided that the fever was probably because of my shallow breathing. I was strongly encouraged to do my breathing exercises and sent to my sister-in-law's house to recuperate.

Every week after that, I was to stop by the plastic surgeon's office and have more saline put in. Just before radiation was to begin, we would drain out all of the saline. Then I would have my six-and-a-half weeks of radiation, after which she'd quickly reinflate the expanders, let them sit for a while, then exchange them for the implants. At least, that was the plan.

What actually happened was that I couldn't tolerate the pain of rapid expansion. I was miserable and depressed. I had gone into the surgery with a chest cold. There had been some debate among the doctors and nurses about whether to continue with the procedure, but they had decided to perform it. My coughing and the pressure of the saline were constantly pulling against the stitches. The expander pushed into my left armpit, leaving me continually feeling like I was leaning heavily on a fence. My arm and hand would tingle and sometimes go numb. I couldn't sleep at night because every position I tried made some part of my body scream in agony.

I finally called my surgical oncologist who asked what pain meds I was taking. I told her that I hadn't been given any. She had me call my plastic surgeon, who informed me that "No one has ever needed pain meds before." I asked her if she'd ever done rapid expansion after bilateral mastectomies before, and she quietly admitted, "No," before offering me a narcotic prescription.

The nights after the mastectomies were my darkest hours. I'd toss and turn trying to find a comfortable, or at least less painful, position. My chest muscles were so tight each breath was a struggle. I had nightmares about buildings collapsing on top of me, of lying on my back trapped under the rubble. At one point I commented miserably to my mother that it might have been better if I had died on the table. At a few points I really wished I had.

But each day got a tiny bit easier.

I remember the morning that I woke up almost refreshed. Instead of the piles of rubble, I'd dreamt that my twenty-pound cat was curled up on my chest. A couple of nights after that, I dreamt that I was leaning back against my Abba and it was only the warm gentle pressure of His healing hands.

Around this time, I found a website called BreastFree. It was full of stories and advice from women who had chosen not to have reconstruction. I devoured every story, and scrolled through every posting. I saw pictures of happy women who had chosen to "go flat," and I suddenly realized that it would be okay if I made that same choice. Though I wouldn't be Barbie, I wouldn't be a freak. I'd simply be human. It helped so much to simply know that I wasn't alone.

I called my plastic surgeon and told her that I wanted the expanders out. "You'll never be able to change your mind. After radiation, you'll never be able to have reconstruction," she warned me, trying to talk me out of my decision. But for once, I had firmly made up my mind, with no doubt whatsoever. This is what I wanted. At the time I didn't even realize that I was taking her first piece of advice to me. But it wouldn't have mattered. This was a place I had to get to on my own. A month and a day after the mastectomies, I had the expanders removed. The surgeon was surprised at how tight the area was, and I was grateful for the freedom to take a deep breath. Yes, I was sad that I wouldn't have breasts, but it was my own choice. This time, I chose to let them go. I gave up any hope of ever being Barbie, and I never regretted that choice.

I did have my prostheses, two sets, for the days I wanted to look "normal." I had pockets sewn into two of my favorite bathing suits so that I could wear them with the prostheses, and I discovered that Lands' End has a line of mastectomy swim-suits. I also found a beautiful pink tank top with spaghetti straps and prostheses pockets in the gift shop at Dana Farber. I began exploring all the clothes stores, looking for nice shirts that I could wear with prostheses, and I learned not to lean over without my hand on my shirt as the weight of the prostheses would drag them away from my chest.

I also had these neat stick-on breasts that I could wear without pockets or a bra and just peel off and stick in the closet at the end of the day. Of course, it feels a bit like peeling off duct tape so I only wore them once.

I bought shirts that cleverly disguised the flatness for the days I didn't want the extra weight and reminder. Scarves camouflage, bows and ruffles distract.

Most days I did wear the prostheses, just because I was so tired of looking at people and wondering if they noticed that I didn't have breasts.

But some days it didn't matter. One day I even went to the beach in a bathing suit without the prostheses. It took a while before I had the courage to take off my cover-up, but nobody gasped at my hideousness. No children started screaming. No conversations stopped so people could gape. I looked around at the people near me, daring them to notice, daring them to comment. But no one did.

I felt a bit freer after that. To wear or not to wear – it was up to me. The prostheses were for me, not for the world at large. I am not required to conform to society. I don't need to have breasts. Life goes on.

I was still me.

Yes, some days I was still really sad. I would stand in front of the mirror and look at my slowly growing hair and my new collection of scars, and cry. This is not what I wanted to do. This is not who I wanted to be.

But some days I couldn't help but laugh at the fears I felt. I fought to live and I'm going to *live*. I determined that I was not going to be chained up by society's idea of what's perfect. I was not going to hide in my home afraid of what might happen next or of what people might be thinking. And I certainly was not going to wear my breasts when exercising. Could Barbie say that?

12 HOLDING MY HEART

I remember having a conversation about saliva with my dental hygienist. Other than brushing my teeth, my dental hygiene had been put on hold during treatment. Somehow I just couldn't convince myself of the necessity of flossing in the face of everything else I was forcing my body to go through. So, when I sat down in her chair and opened my mouth, it had been a while.

She was impressed with how healthy my gums looked. Many cancer patients struggle with mouth sores as chemotherapy can cause a decrease in saliva production. I, however, have always had an overabundance of saliva which tends to keep my teeth clean and healthy. I never had a single mouth sore during treatment...

When I was twelve years old, my parents finally made it to West Africa as missionaries. I remember when the plane landed and I looked out that window at the fog-covered land. It looked so cold outside. But when we climbed down the stairs from the plane the heat sat on us thick, damp, and heavy. I was excited, but very scared as well.

My parents drove my brother and me two hours up north to the boarding school we'd be staying at. Other missionaries had told them that a clean, quick goodbye was the easiest, so my father carried my suitcase into my new room and set it on the floor. We all hugged each other and then they were gone. I sat down on my suitcase and cried.

That's one of those mental images that can still bring tears. A little girl sitting on a suitcase, alone and crying. But my Abba was with me that day, holding my heart.

My mom came with me to my second mammogram. She drove me to the biopsy. She sat with me during my first chemo. And my second. And my third. Test after test. MRIs, CT scans, surgeries, consults. Mom was there beside me the whole way.

When the mission my parents worked for told them it was time to go back to Africa, Mom said no. She knew that her place was here with me. My parents chose to take a ten-month leave of absence to sit down by my side. They gave up their paychecks and lost their health insurance. They stepped forward with no security – other than that of knowing that they were walking in the center of the Father's will.

And God honored their decision. Meals were provided, funds were donated. Friends helped out. No one went hungry and all the bills got paid.

And when I saw what my mom was willing to do for me – for me! – my heart finally understood how much she loves me. How much she always loved me.

Now when I picture that little girl sitting on a suitcase alone at boarding school, I'm very sorry for the pain she's holding, but I'm not crying. Because I know how much my mom loves me. I know that she once dropped everything to come and sit by my side, to hold my hand and fetch me a glass of ice water, to drive my manual transmission in Boston traffic during rush hour, because she loves me. It took a detour through cancer to teach me that.

What a small price to pay for such a priceless truth.

I am loved. More than I can fathom.

When I was fourteen years old, I was diagnosed with scoliosis, a slight curvature of my spine. As with all diagnoses, there were good and bad things that came with this. I was placed in a special gym class, with the two other girls in my school who had scoliosis, and we learned the exercises that we were supposed to do daily for the rest of our lives. This was a bad thing. I was also told not to jog or participate in regular gym classes. This was a good thing.

I wasn't happy with the diagnosis.

I didn't want to be crooked. I didn't want to be different.

I remember praying for months that God would take it away. I knew beyond a shadow of a doubt that He could – my faith was in an all-powerful God Who could do miracles with no effort. The questions arose when I wondered if He would do any of those miracles for *me*. I prayed that He'd make my scoliosis go away. But He didn't.

Before my cancer diagnosis, I went to a physical therapist for my back pain. He did some measurements and determined that one leg was three quarters of an inch shorter than the other, which threw off my hips and caused most of the pain. I got a prescription for walking shoes (along with strong encouragement to use them) and another list of exercises to do.

I am all for exercises. Well, somewhat all for some of them. However, when the doctor told me back when I was fourteen that the exercises would not make the problem go away, I never really got into a routine of doing them. They hurt. Now I better understand the concept of preventative practice. The exercises wouldn't make the scoliosis go away, but they could keep it from getting worse.

Over the years, I've learned to deal with the scoliosis. It's such a small thing in the hugeness of my life. One shoulder is lower than the other. I've learned to adapt. I instinctively carry my bags on the other shoulder so that I'm not always dropping them. I only buy tank tops with adjustable straps. I do my exercises when my back hurts enough to remind me that I am supposed to be doing them. I'm definitely over it.

But sometimes I wondered why God didn't answer me back then.

Now I know.

My cancer was Her2nu driven. Her2nu is a protein that wraps around the cancer cells and tells them to ignore any signals to die and to just keep growing. Herceptin is a biologic that attaches to the receptors and blocks the protein's message. Until Herceptin was discovered there was no cure, but now it's one of the most easily treated types of breast cancer.

The down side is that this same protein is wrapped around our hearts.

Throughout my treatments, I had periodic scans to make sure no damage was being done to my heart. The lab technician would take a small vial of my blood and add a radioactive tag to it. Then they would inject the blood back into my body and watch how it flowed through my heart. I would get to lie on a table with a large camera about an inch from my chest taking pictures of my heart pumping this blood throughout its chambers. Each test took about a half hour. I had to lie absolutely still because anytime I moved, the camera would start over.

Sometimes it was hard to lie calmly there on that table, with a huge box less than an inch from my face covering me with its dark shadow. But God often used these times to remind me to be still and know Him. To remember in the dark shadows all the promises He'd whispered in the sunlight. All I had to do was rest. He was holding my heart.

At the first heart scan, my test score came back as 75+, super healthy. At each scan after that, the numbers dropped; steadily, but not significantly. The "book" says that if the numbers drop by sixteen points then the treatments should be stopped. Just before my last treatment, my estimated LVEF was 60%. I explained to my oncologist that this wasn't technically sixteen points, merely 15+. My oncologist laughed, and then responded that even if it was the full sixteen points, 60% is still an acceptable number. I was merely healthy, no longer super healthy. And we decided to squeeze in the last treatment. I was glad. I really don't know how much difference one treatment can make, but I do know how nervous (downright frightened) I would have been that the cancer would come back if I didn't finish the treatment program.

But that isn't the end of the story.

After thirteen rounds of Herceptin, we took a break for the mastectomies and then radiation. The first step for radiation was to have a computer-generated 3D image made of my body to create the radiation program. This program included three fields of radiation, all aimed at different layers of the skin, bone, and muscle where the tumor bed had been. One of those fields included the chest wall and the heart. Now, I don't know too much about radiation, but one kind surgeon was happy to point out that for some odd reason while radiation destroys cancerous cells, it also has a tendency to cause cancer in healthy cells. The goal is to minimize the radiation sent to healthy organs. One of the main reasons I couldn't have full expanders in during radiation was that the angle of radiation would have to be changed to go around the expanders and this usually resulted in more radiation to the heart. My heart had already been exposed to four rounds of Adriamycin and Cytoxan and a handful of Herceptin.

I remember the appointment when I met with my radiation oncology nurse and asked her if the radiation would touch my heart. She left the room to find that answer. When she came back, she said that it would touch the very tip of my heart. "However," she went on to point out, "everyone's anatomy is a little bit different." My heart is further back from my chest wall than most people's, so it will be getting a lot less radiation than normally expected, and so very minimal damage.

After a quiet moment digesting this, I asked her if my scoliosis could have affected the placement of my heart. "Yes," she answered with a smile. "It very well could have."

God wasn't ignoring me when I was fourteen. He was just answering all of the prayers we'd be praying nineteen years later. He was holding my heart.

13 RADIATION REACTION

I chose to do radiation locally, instead of at Dana Farber. Somehow, even though I love road trips, the thought of driving for three hours every day for six-and-a-half weeks was not very appealing.

I think the most painful part of radiation was the tattoos. After a series of CT scans and X-rays used to create a specialized computer program geared toward my body and my cancer, they had to make sure that the radiation hit the exact same spot every time. To do this, the nurse made six blue dots on my skin. She grabbed a pin, dipped it into a puddle of ink, and then stabbed, wiggled, and dug it into my skin until there was a blue spot the size she wanted. Six times. At the end of all of my radiation treatment, my oncologist wrote a note on his prescription pad giving me permission to tattoo over them. On my one-year anniversary from diagnosis, I got a tattoo of a butterfly on my chest, with its antenna wrapping confidently around the most prominent blue dot.

My first radiation was on February 13, 2008, almost two months after my bilateral mastectomies. I arrived at the hospital and registered on the first floor, before heading up to the second floor to changed into a johnny and have a seat in the waiting room. I met my newest nurse and made some new friends.

It was usually a twenty- to thirty-minute wait every day, and it was always the same group of people in the waiting room. Sometimes we sat quietly and read magazines, though after the first six visits I had read most of the waiting room copies from cover to cover. Some days the TV was on and we'd watch soap operas. Sometimes I'd grab a snack from the mini-fridge (they had

Ensure and chocolate pudding). Often we'd talk – about cancer, about family members and dentist appointments. We always got called out in the same order, and we always wished each other well on the way out.

I very quickly fell into the routine. I would leave work a little after 1:00 and drive to the Peter Levine Cancer Center off Belmont Street. I'd park in the garage, then go up the outside steps into the center.

On the first day of each month, I had to stop at the first floor and register. All of the other days, I could go straight up to the second floor, announce my name at the front desk, then head to the changing room to put on my johnny. Yes, *my* johnny. One of the best things I did during my radiation days was to buy my own johnny. I'd found a great website by a couple of sisters where I could purchase my own instead of borrowing one from the hospital. Although there were three patterns to choose from at the hospital, there were only two sizes: big and way too big. And they came in two variations: missing strings or knotted strings. For $70, I was able to get a beautiful pink Velcro johnny that actually let me feel pretty when walking down the hallway instead of embarrassingly half naked. Even something as simple as being able to decide what to wear can have a huge effect on your self-esteem. I think everyone should have their own johnny.

After slipping into my johnny I would sit in one of the six chairs in the tiny, open waiting room and visit. Sometimes I'd chat with the woman waiting for her mother. Her mother was a sweetheart who'd made beautiful heart pins for everyone on Valentine's Day. I still have mine in a drawer in my bureau. Sometimes I'd talk with the old couple who always arrived a little later. His appointment was right after mine. We all had such different stories, but we were all cheerful. Sometimes that little waiting room rang with laughter.

When it was my turn, I'd walk down the hallway past a door a foot thick and into a large cold room. I'd climb up onto a table and grab the two handles over my head. A technician would slide a pillow under my left arm, drape a heated blanket over me, raise my table, then walk out of the room, closing the door behind her. Then I would just wait. Pray. Think. Wait some more. Pray some more. It was only fifteen minutes, but some days it felt like so much longer than that.

Most of the time, it seems like absolutely nothing is going on. Then the machine moves a little and makes a loud buzzing sound. Sometimes I thought I could feel my skin tingle a bit.

Then, eventually, the technicians would come back into the room, lift the machine, and lower the bed. I'd get up, change back into my clothes, say goodbye to the gentleman and his wife, stop at the front desk for a parking voucher, and go home. In and out within forty-five minutes. Thirty-two times.

One radiation day stands out in my memory – the day they forgot a blanket. The technician got me settled, raised the table, and walked out swinging the door shut behind her. I didn't even have a chance to call out before the door closed. I lay there, flat on my back with my hands stretched over my head, with my scars-instead-of-breasts fully exposed to everyone who walked by the monitor in the station off the hallway.

It wasn't that I was cold. The heated blankets weren't only for the heat. They covered me up. Without them, I was exposed. I felt helpless. I felt hopeless. All of my secrets bared to the world. I didn't mind people seeing my scars, I just wanted it to be my choice.

The seconds dragged by as tears pooled in my eyes and I wavered back and forth between feeling shamed and feeling angry. That was one of the only times during my cancer detour that I truly felt that I had lost my dignity.

Radiation continued. Some days it was a short session, only fifteen minutes lying still on the table. Other days it was a little bit longer as they took X-rays and photographs to be sure that everything was still centered correctly.

By March, my skin was beginning to get very itchy and blistered. I remember when the technician looked at me sadly, shaking his head, and mumbled that it was only going to get worse. I gripped the bars above my head, closed my eyes, and prayed my way through another session.

Some of the sessions I actually slept through.

By the twenty-second session, it hurt to move my arm. My armpit was dark red and the blisters were swollen and itchy. My arm was beginning to get puffy with lymph fluid and I began wearing a compression sleeve and glove. The doctor decided that from now on I'd have to visit with him before each session so that he could decide if my skin could handle another treatment. They have this amazing cream that will clear up the blisters right away, only you can't use it if you're going to have radiation. If the irritation got bad enough to skip a couple of doses of radiation, they would give me the cream to clear up the blisters.

I remember when the nurse asked me how bad the pain was. I've always found it difficult to put a number on pain. It definitely hurt less than labor. Much less than a bilateral mastectomy, but a bit more than a snakebite. Does that make it a five?

On my twenty-third radiation day, I sat on an exam table, holding my arm up high, with two doctors and a nurse gazing intently at my armpit. It was one

of those surreal moments in life. These things don't really happen to normal
people, do they? My oncologist was on vacation, so a substitute doctor had to
make the call. After a bit of debate, we squeezed in another treatment. The
reaction was decidedly uncomfortable but we had just finished radiating the
supraclavicular field, so they decided it was safe to continue. What they didn't
realize was that the blistered area was in two of the three radiation fields and it
continued to get exposure to the radiation.

Finally, on March 25, they called a halt to the treatments. By this time,
there was a bit of nasty yellow stuff seeping from the blisters. My nurse made
a grumpy face when she saw it. She disappeared down the hallway and
returned with a tiny canister of white cream and the substitute doctor. He
asked how many days I'd like off. I answered, "As many as I can get." He
gave me three. I used the cream every day, and the reaction cleared up quickly.

Reaction. That's what those icky, drippy blisters are called. I made the
mistake of calling it a burn once, and from the oncologist's reaction you'd
have thought it was the worst four-letter word he'd ever heard. I was afraid he
was going to wash my mouth out with soap.

When I got home and told my family this new tidbit, my son started
laughing. "What about *dead*?" he asked with a grin. "Isn't *dead* worse than
burn?" Oh, the mouth on that boy.

After my short break, my doctor returned from vacation and we finished
off the rest of the radiation sessions. As we neared the end, he informed me
that it's normal for patients to feel sad when the treatments end. They felt
good as long as they were actively doing something to keep the cancer at bay,
and it's hard to suddenly stop and just wait. He then assured me that even
though I wasn't driving in every day for my daily dose of radiation, the
radiation I'd already received would still be running through my body fighting
cancer long after the active treatments had stopped.

I think another piece of the sadness is simply losing the daily fellowship
with other cancer survivors. Letting go of the routine. Knowing that you'll
probably never see them again. Wondering if their cancer will come back.
Wondering if yours will.

My last "glow treatment" was on April 8, 2008. I got off the table, thanked
and hugged the nurses and technicians, received my parking voucher, and
drove home. My mom and I went out and got pedicures to celebrate. I had
butterflies painted on my big toes. Then, it was back to life as normal.

I had continued teaching throughout my cancer treatments, with small
breaks for recovery after surgeries. During radiation I went down to half days,

teaching in the morning, then going out for lunch before driving in to Worcester. On April 9, I walked into my classroom and one excited student asked, "Is this the day you stay?" "Yes." I answered, as I settled down at my desk. "Today is the day I stay."

I don't miss those radiation days. I don't miss the lurchy elevator, or the *National Geographic* magazine I'd read six times. I don't miss having to push through the cloud of smoke and smokers huddled on the outside stairs by the parking garage. I don't really miss the smiling technicians who gave me hugs on my last day, or the doctors and nurses, or the tiny table that moves up and down. Or the soap operas on the new TV, or the little fridge stocked with Ensure and pudding. I don't even miss the free hot chocolate. And I definitely don't miss those little, invisible radiation beams (which I hope didn't miss any remaining cancer!).

What *do* I miss? One of the technicians called it. On my way out, after my last treatment, she gave me a hug and a smile. Then she said, "You may not miss us, but you'll miss our heated blankets." She was right.

But, as my mother pointed out, whenever I get nostalgic I can drop a blanket in the dryer for a few minutes. No need to go back. Life moves forward.

But sometimes we want to go back, don't we? Back to the days before the cancer was found. Back to the days before the surgery. Back to childhood. Back to write-your-best-moment-here.

The hope and encouragement here? Heaven is better. God has promised that. It's going to be better than anything I can ask, or even dream up. Even better than sitting under a heated blanket while eating a hot fudge sundae. With a good book. Next to a friend.

Yes. Even better than that.

With that in front of you, who'd want to go back? I suppose there's still the fear of the unknown in the way, but God knows it. And I know God. Well, I'm working on getting to know Him.

And even better than that, He knows me.

14 BEADS ON A WIRE

One day while my mom and I were eating lunch in the Dana Farber cafeteria, I found an article about a bead program they have for children. Every time a child comes in for a cancer treatment, they can head up to the children's room and pick out a bead. I decided that I wanted to do that myself.

I went to the Charlton Mills Box Factory Outlet and Craft Emporium and spent $40 on glass beads. I cut a piece of copper wire, fastened one end to a keychain, and began stringing on beads for the treatments I'd already done.

Each blue teardrop is a surgery. Each pink teardrop is a cancer diagnosis. Each benign report is represented by a purple cross. The thirty-six sparkly white droplets are my thirty-six days of radiation. Cat's eyes for the CT scans. Purple stars for nights spent in the hospital. Pretty purple beads for Taxol and small pink ones for Herceptin. The white ones are Abraxane, and the pretty red and yellow swirly ones represent the Adriamycin/Cytoxan infusions. Black cylinders, of course, for the MRIs.

Every step of my cancer journey is strung on that five-foot long piece of wire. It's a story told in sparkly glass gems.

But here's the neat part: I didn't near the end of the wire until I neared the end of the journey. I celebrated the end of radiation, finished up physical therapy for my shoulder and chest muscles, had my last heart scan, and endured my last chemo infusion. Then, finally, I had the port removed. It was finished. That was the last step in my treatment program, and there was just enough wire left to slide on that last blue tear-drop and roll up the end to keep the beads from falling off.

That day way back in the beginning when I'd cut off a piece of wire, I cut the wire to the exact length it needed to be. God knew how many beads I would need. He knew from the beginning every step I would be taking. None of this took Him by surprise. I find a lot of peace in that.

One hundred sixty-six beads on a copper wire – and not one of them was outside of God's plan for me.

ONE HUNDRED SIXTY-SIX BEADS ON A WIRE

1. Me
2. Mammogram
3. Ultrasound
4. Biopsy
5. Diagnosis
6. MRI
7. X-ray
8. CT scan
9. Gene test
10. Sentinel node biopsy
11. Donated hair
12. Bone scan
13. MRI
14. Heart scan
15. AC – first chemo
16. Diagnosis – in the nodes
17. Ultrasound
18. Negative gene test results
19. CT scan
20. Four nights in the hospital
21. Shaved head
22. MRI-guided biopsy
23. PowerPort
24. AC #2
25. Neulasta shot
26. Benign results
27. Butterfly day – family cookout, Wes turned 13!
28. AC #3
29. Neulasta shot
30. AC #4
31. Neulasta shot
32. Ultrasound
33. Relay for Life '07
34. Butterfly day – Six Flags
35. Taxol #1
36. Herceptin #1
37. Heart scan
38. Taxol #2
39. Herceptin #2
40. Uncle Marvin died of prostate cancer

41. Taxol #3
42. Herceptin #3
43. Taxol #4
44. Herceptin #4
45. Butterfly day – teacher appreciation basket
46. Taxol #5
47. Herceptin #5
48. X-ray
49. Heart scan
50. Abraxane #1
51. Herceptin #6
52. Butterfly day – Apologetix concert
53. MRI
54. Abraxane #2
55. Herceptin #7
56. Chemo-induced menopause
57. Abraxane #3
58. Herceptin #8
59. Butterfly day – scrapbooking retreat
60. Abraxane #4
61. Herceptin #9
62. Butterfly day – finished my sitting room
63. Abraxane #5
64. Herceptin #10
65. Butterfly day – Thanksgiving
66. Abraxane #6
67. Herceptin #11
68. Abraxane #7
69. Herceptin #12
70. Butterfly day – Christmas shopping at Cracker Barrel
71. Heart scan
72. Bilateral mastectomies
73. One night in the hospital
74. Chest X-ray
75. One night in the hospital
76. Herceptin #13
77. Pathology results – left cancer, right benign
78. Started Caring Bridge website
79. Period
80. Herceptin #14
81. Expanders removed
82. CT scan
83. Moles removed

84. Butterfly day – back to work
85. Herceptin #15
86. X-ray
87. Butterfly day – carving and bead story
88. Benign moles
89. Radiation
90. Butterfly day – Valentine's Day
91. Radiation
92. Radiation
93. Radiation
94. Radiation
95. Radiation
96. Radiation
97. Radiation
98. Nichol's fundraiser
99. Radiation
100. Herceptin #16
101. Radiation
102. Radiation
103. Butterfly day – scrapbooking retreat
104. Friend died of cancer
105. Radiation
106. Radiation
107. Radiation
108. Radiation
109. Radiation
110. Radiation
111. Radiation
112. Radiation
113. Radiation
114. Radiation
115. Physical therapy
116. Radiation
117. Physical therapy
118. Radiation
119. Radiation
120. Radiation
121. Physical therapy
122. Herceptin #17
123. Butterfly day – my birthday in Boston
124. Physical therapy
125. Physical therapy
126. Radiation

127.Ultrasound
128.Radiation
129.Radiation
130.Radiation
131.Radiation
132.Physical therapy
133.Radiation
134.Radiation
135.Radiation
136.Radiation
137.Butterfly day – last radiation celebration
138.Physical therapy
139.Herceptin #18
140.Physical therapy
141.Physical therapy
142.Physical therapy
143.Herceptin #19
144.Physical therapy
145.Physical therapy
146.Herceptin #20
147.Butterfly day – breast fitting
148.Physical therapy
149.Butterfly day – one year tattoo
150.Physical therapy
151.Herceptin #21
152.Physical therapy
153.Herceptin #22
154.Herceptin #23
155.Butterfly day – hair cut one year from shaving
156.Physical therapy
157.Heart scan
158.Herceptin #24
159.Physical therapy
160.Physical therapy
161.Heart scan
162.Herceptin #25
163.Physical therapy
164.Herceptin #26 last chemo!!!
165.Butterfly day – Relay for Life '08
166.Port removal

15 BUTTERFLY DAYS

My grandmother once told me that butterflies were healing thoughts from above. Every card she gave me after my diagnosis had at least one butterfly on it. And there were usually several butterfly stickers scattered on the envelope. I remember sitting in my chair by the lake at camp, tired and sore from chemo, watching a caterpillar slowly crawl by. "That's almost a butterfly," I thought. And I smiled.

There are eighteen butterfly beads on my wire. Each one represents a special day. A day full of laughter, or simply fun. A day when cancer was little and LIFE was big. A day that I want to remember just as clearly as the chemos and the surgeries. A day where something happened that was just as important to my health and survival as removing the cancer from my body. What would be the point in only dwelling on the treatments that touched my body? Why not also mark the ones that touched my soul?

My first butterfly day was our family cookout. The whole family gathered in my uncle's back yard to talk and visit. We ate macaroni salad and savored Dixie cups of ice-cream. We celebrated all of the July birthdays – my son had just turned thirteen! I was bald by this time, but no one cared. I just sat in a lawn chair surrounded by family, and celebrated life.

My second butterfly day was a day full of surprises. It was the morning after my first Relay for Life. I had walked nine miles the night before, but still dragged myself out of bed to go to the closing ceremonies that morning. When I got there, I discovered that I had won a raffle basket full of miscellaneous treasures.

After the closing ceremonies, I went out to eat with my mom and a friend of mine. As we were devouring our desserts, I received a phone call from another friend. She was at Six Flags with a college group. Four people never showed up, so if I wanted to join them she had four extra tickets for us. We drove home to pick up my son and then headed out to spend the rest of the day at Six Flags.

When I finally returned home that evening, I had just enough energy left to open my gift basket and sort through it. I found something special for everyone in there. The dark chocolate went to my father. The lotion went to Mom. Grammy got the teas and smelly soaps. My son got some neat little gadget. I kept a couple of knickknacks and hid the Hide-a-Key. I don't remember where…

I slept well that night, fully assured that God was in control and that everything would be all right. Not merely because I'd had a good day, and not because I'd gotten so much free stuff. But because I had laughed. Because I had played. Because cancer had been put in the backseat for a while.

There were so many other butterfly days – the day I won the teacher appreciation basket at Borders. I'd been having a sad day when they called me. My mom asked why I was winning things all of a sudden. I grinned at her and said, "It's because Abba knew I needed some cheering up." He's good like that!

Then there was the day I went to an Apologetix concert with a friend, the two scrapbooking retreats I went on, the day we finished painting and organizing the sitting room and I had my own special space to retreat to when the treatments took their toll. And, of course, there was Thanksgiving, and then Christmas.

Oh, and the day I went back to work almost two months after my mastectomies! As I walked into the school building, I caught a few words out of the corner of my eye: "Book," "Fair," "Monica." I quickly backpedaled to take another look at the marquis. Right under the ad for the upcoming bookfair, were the words, "Welcome back, Monica."

With a smile I entered the building and headed slowly up the stairs to my classroom. The first teacher I encountered had a beautiful pink scarf wrapped around her neck. We exchanged greetings and I kept walking. The second teacher I bumped into also wore one. When I got to my classroom, I found another one folded neatly on my desk.

Shortly after that, I was paged down to the office. As I made my way down, I passed the cafeteria – and stopped short. All of the staff members were in there, seated around a table of breakfast goodies, each one wearing a hand-knitted pink scarf. My heart overflowed. It was a definite butterfly day.

Then there was Valentine's Day when I was overwhelmed with goodies from coworkers and friends who just wanted to take one more opportunity to remind me that I was loved. And my breast-fitting appointment got a butterfly, too.

There's just something surreal about going breast shopping with your mom. I think part of me was irrationally hoping that I would get my new prosthesis and everything would go back to normal. But another part of me was worrying – what if I couldn't find any that I liked? What if my insurance would only pay for the bottom of the line, uncomfortable ones? What if they didn't look right? What if...

When we got to the appointment, the salesclerk checked on her computer and asked if I was sure that I was supposed to be there. Apparently Mary had blocked out that afternoon for another task. Then she entered my name into a second computer by the register and found that I did indeed have an appointment.

"Not a problem," Mary said, as she led us into her back room. It was around that time I realized that I'd left my prostheses prescriptions at home. Mary again said, "Not a problem." I could just mail them to her later.

Mary's first question for me was, "What size bra did you wear?"

I briefly considered all of the witty responses I could make before settling on the truth. "I never wore one." Her jaw dropped and she began laughing as she measured my chest. Then she asked me what size I wanted to be.

After a bit of discussion, we decided to start with an A. I could always change my mind later. My insurance would pay for anything I had a prescription for, so I would just have to call my surgeon if I needed to make a change.

Then she pulled out the breasts.

There are little ones – sizes zero through three are A's – and big ones. Just for fun, I pulled out a size nine. It was bigger than my head and completely covered my chest. I'm not sure where I would have put the second one.

There were also sticky ones that could be worn with strapless bras. Very sticky ones. Mary recommended that I wait on those, as pulling it off every night would irritate my still healing radiated skin. I did end up getting a pair of these later. There are also clear ones for swimming (as opposed the normal tan and brown ones).

I chose five bras and the size three regular prostheses. She only had one in stock so she had to place an order. My breasts came in the mail a few days later.

I left Mary's office feeling lighthearted and hopeful. Life didn't suddenly become right again, but I realized that not all of it was wrong.

Another butterfly day was the day my hair had finally grown long enough to be cut – my first haircut – exactly one year from the day it had been shaved. Also, the day I got my first tattoo, the day I went to my second Relay for Life, and the day I had my last radiation session. Another was the day a beautiful hand-carved cross came in the mail, a cross with Jesus standing before it, holding His arms out to me. The thought behind it was just as beautiful as the cross itself – the carver had been thinking of me and praying for me with each knife stroke. It's hanging on the wall in my sitting room now, reminding me of God's love for each one of us.

But my favorite butterfly day was my birthday. It was a chemo day, and my mom, two friends, and I piled into the car to make the trek to Boston. We met with the nurse, visited with my doctor, then headed upstairs where we laughed our way through my Herceptin infusion. After that we explored Boston on foot following the freedom trail and carefully avoiding birds and squirrels. We stopped by and toured Old Ironsides, splashed each other from an indoor fountain, took a zillion pictures, and then went to the top of the Prudential Center for hamburgers and fries.

Surviving cancer isn't just chemo, surgery, and radiation. It isn't only nausea and pain. It isn't simply trying to be cheerful and positive. It *is* being cheerful and positive. It's laughing when something is funny. It's looking for something fun to do between appointments. It's noticing all of the people around you. It's putting down the camera and going to play with your son. It's tapping your toes when you don't have the energy to dance. It's remembering the butterfly days just as vividly as the treatments.

EIGHTEEN BUTTERFLY DAYS

16 TWO LITTLE PEARLS

My port was removed on September 11, 2008. I was under conscious sedation, though I only remember the part when he suddenly said, "Monica, hold your breath now." Then there was a slight tugging sensation as he gently pulled the cord out of my jugular and chest. Now there's just a fading one-and-a-half-inch scar to remind me of those chemo days.

One day, the nurse who was accessing my port commented on my butterfly tattoo. Then he said that when this was all done I should get a tattoo where the port had been. "Something really painful, like a wasp," he said with a smile.

And I might. Or maybe just a needle that looks like it's pulling a pink ribbon as if it's sewing up the scar. It's fun finding ways to make cancer's leftovers beautifully mine.

On Valentine's Day 2009 I found two new lumps on the incision where my left breast had been. I spent a couple of days plotting out how exactly I would craft the message telling the world that my cancer had returned. I was scolded by one friend for the way I told people the first time around. Apparently, when someone asks, "How are you?" it's not socially acceptable to simply answer, "I have cancer." This time, I decided I could soften the blow a little bit and say, "My cancer's back, but you'll be fine."

Finally, I called my medical oncologist and told him about the new lumps. He invited me up for a visit. After he felt the lumps, he went off in search of a surgeon. The surgeon took a careful feel and decided that it was just scar tissue. The spots were too small to do any imaging on, so our options were to wait or to biopsy. He told me to come back in two weeks.

When I went back two weeks later, he again declared them benign, but we decided to do a biopsy anyway. "So I can prove that I'm right," he told me with a grin.

I had the biopsy on March 13. This surgery was done under local anesthesia. I got to the Ambulatory Treatment Center, changed into a johnny and a bathrobe, and curled up on hospital bed to wait. This place wasn't nearly as formal as most of the hospitals I'd been in. People here seemed relaxed and happy. However, there was an odd tense moment when a doctor across the hall was trying to get the sink to work. Have you ever seen someone kicking a stingy vending machine? I told my friend that if she heard any loud banging sounds while I was in surgery, she was to come in and get me immediately.

My doctor stopped by to check if my lumps were still there. They were, so he drew little blue circles around them. Then I signed my consent forms, got off the hospital bed, and walked behind him into the operating room, where I climbed up onto another table. They put a pillow beneath my knees, and one nurse scrubbed my chest while another put a sticky patch on my arm that would send an electric current though my body to help stop the bleeding. They gave me a heated blanket, then placed a folded blue tarp on my feet and slowly unrolled it up over my body. When they came to my neck, they hung the end of the tarp from two poles, keeping my face out in the open but sheltered. The surgeon then clipped a green sterile handle onto the light so he could move it around, and they began.

"You'll feel a slight pinch and a burn," he told me. I braced myself. "And now another one." But because of my previous surgeries, my skin was desensitized and I hadn't even felt the first one.

I guess I had expected that they would simply cut the scar open, pull out the offending lumps, and then sew me back up. However, it was more like they cut me open, made some jokes about there not really being any George Clooneys at that hospital in Chicago, talked about the beautiful weather outside, and *searched* for the lumps. My surgeon was more excited than a five year old on an Easter egg hunt when he finally found one. Then he sewed me back up (I could hear the snips when he cut the sutures) and moved over to the other spot.

He described the lumps as "two small pearls" and said that they both looked really benign. Then he added that when we get the negative results, I can meet with a plastic surgeon and begin looking at reconstruction. He also suggested I meet with him one more time to discuss the other five tattoos I need to cover up the rest of the radiation dots.

I really liked the idea of calling those lumps pearls. I liked the idea that my body could take an irritation, probably just a piece of undissolved suture – a cancer leftover – and turn it into a beautiful little pearl.

The wakeful surgery was easier to recover from than the sleep-through ones. It seems to be the anesthesia that wipes me out and makes me sick. At first, everything was trial and error and it seemed that each surgery was just another chance to find out what not to do. But by the last surgery we pretty much had it down to a science.

No Decadron or nausea patch – they both make me nauseous. No iodine – itchy rash. No parabens – another itchy rash. No adhesive – that one left an inch long blister on my back. Too much Benadryl makes me loopy, but a little in the cocktail seems to help. We've learned a lot over these past seven years of experimentation.

I now know more about me than I ever thought there was to learn. And I know that I can make pearls.

17 GETTING BUMPS

I went flat for about a year and a half. It was good. Most of the time I was content. I wore my prostheses on weekdays, and went flat most weekends. But each morning, when I took them out of the box, I remembered everything again. It was a constant reminder of what I'd lost. I never got used to the scars on my chest. On the days when I chose not to wear the prostheses, I had to search through my closet for shirts that weren't designed with breasts in mind. Yes, ruffles and scarves can distract from the absence of bumps, but they can't take away the big empty pucker in a fitted blouse.

I never regretted the choice to go flat. But one day I knew it was time to move on. So I decided to get new bumps.

I found a plastic surgeon who sat me down and told me the options. We could use my stomach muscles and make two small breasts, though he really didn't recommend this because of the amount of healing involved. The other option was a latissimus dorsi flap reconstruction – to use my back muscle and make a pocket on the left side to compensate for the radiated skin and muscle. Then we could slip in some expanders and slowly stretch the skin to whatever size we wanted. He assured me that the other back muscles would all compensate for the loss and it would have no negative impact on my scoliosis.

It would be a one- to two-hour surgery, with one to two days in the hospital and a two- to three-week recovery time. After that, we could expand at any rate I was comfortable with. He didn't believe in rapid expansion because it's often not tolerated well. At this point he paused, looked at me, and made it very clear that he could not give me my old breasts back. I nodded.

I went home to ponder and pray, and decided to go for it.

I had reconstructive surgery on October 7, 2009. Before the surgery, the phlebotomist numbed up my right hand and took his time accessing a vein. He told me they'd use that one to put me to sleep, then get a new one going. When I woke up after the surgery, there was an IV in my right foot. I also had pinpricks inside my elbow, one at my wrist, and a large bruise around another pinprick on the side of my arm. Thankfully I slept through all of that poking!

It took my surgeon four hours to cut a chunk of healthy skin and muscle out of my back and tunnel it over to make a pocket on my left side. Then he slid in the empty expanders and sewed everything back up.

They used the IV in my hand during the two nights in the hospital, though it kept clogging and it hurt each time they flushed it. The nurse was determined to keep getting "one more" dose of antibiotics through it. They began taking my blood pressure on my right thigh, and the IV actually lasted until I was discharged from the hospital on Friday morning.

After the surgery, I was absolutely miserable. When I first sat up to get dressed, my nurse handed me a pillow and told me to hold it tightly against my stomach and chest. Not really sure why, I accepted the pillow and had just put it against my stomach when the nausea hit. I clung to that pillow like it was the only thing holding all of my stitches in place as I threw up into the bucket he held near my mouth.

I kept wondering why I'd asked for this surgery and wishing I could go back and undo it. The incisions hurt so much, and I felt that I looked so miserably hideous. My plastic surgeon assured me that this was just a stage. It was not the end result.

At my one-month follow-up appointment, I had the option of putting in 250 ccs of saline or not doing any at all because, as he frequently reminded me, we had all the time in the world. I opted for the 250. I went back every week after that to get more saline pumped in. He would use a little magnet to find the expanders' ports, and then a needle and syringe to insert the saline. We took our time. One week we only added a little bit because I had another cold and had been coughing a lot.

My surgeon used to joke that men shouldn't have his job because their tendency is to keep going bigger. He started calling me DeeDee after that. It was my job to decide when we were done. After each expansion, I was to go home, put on a t-shirt and decide if we'd reached the size I wanted. After a while, I found that it became painful the first couple of days after an expansion, a bit like a pulled muscle. That was how I finally knew we'd reached the size I wanted to be.

On February 11, 2009, I had a quick day surgery to pull out the expanders and put in silicone implants, but we weren't done yet. We then had to wait six months after the surgery for any swelling to go down before we would really know the results of the surgery. What we *could* tell was that one breast was significantly higher than the other. I was given a Velcro band to wrap across my chest that would slowly push that higher breast down. Unfortunately, at the next appointment we discovered that while it had successfully moved the high breast down, it had also nudged the lower one further down.

It was hard not to be discouraged during this time. I had hoped the surgery would make everything normal again. I knew it wouldn't, couldn't, give me back my old breasts, but I guess I was expecting – well, I really don't know what I was expecting. But it wasn't this. I wasn't prepared for such obvious deformity, for having to pull out all the old baggy clothes and scarves again. I hadn't thought it would be worse than being flat and having to wear prostheses.

On December 20, 2009, I had a second day surgery. This time the surgeon swapped out the implants for a set 100 ccs bigger and changed the low-profile implant on the left to a medium profile. He also took some spare fat from my belly, cleaned it up, and injected it around the left implant to fill in some of the dents from the mastectomy. This time I had to wear a girdle to encourage my stomach to heal flat after the fat graft. And again, we waited six months.

By this point I was definitely becoming discouraged. Even though my stomach benefitted from the fat graft, it seemed that after each surgery my breasts were off by a little more. But if you ever need cheering up, I know a guy. He's a plumber friend of mine, who very kindly offered to let my surgeon borrow his level for the next surgery. Fortunately, it wasn't needed.

I had my next surgery during summer vacation, on July 26, 2011. This one was another fat graft, taking fat from my upper thighs, since there wasn't much left on my stomach. I knew what to expect this time, which really didn't help too much as fat grafts are a lot more painful then they sound. Also, since he'd taken fat from my thighs, I had to wear a girdle that went from my belly button to my knees. Did I mention it was July? I did my best to endure the heat and began another six-month waiting period.

By October, it began to look like the implant on the right was slipping over to the side. We weren't sure if it had popped or if the muscle had ripped and the implant had shifted. My surgeon was quick to assure me that even if the implant had ruptured, I was in no danger of silicone poisoning. Today's silicone implants are made of a Swedish fish consistency. If you chop off the head, you simply have a head and a tail, no dangerous silicone leaking into the bloodstream.

We waited and watched the implant for a month, before scheduling an MRI to double check. The results came back normal. Around this time I also found two new lumps which I pointed out to my surgeon.

On February 11, 2012, I had another surgery. My plastic surgeon looked at both implants, removed a bit of scar tissue, drained the left pocket of built-up fluid, and biopsied my two lumps. He sent in the lumps and fluid for testing, put me on antibiotics, and left in a drain to take care of any extra fluid.

Fortunately, all of the biopsies came back benign. Unfortunately, either the painkillers or the antibiotic made me wretchedly sick for three days after the surgery. I think I broke the whole list of post-op rules as soon as I got home, because I just didn't have the time or energy to discover a way to throw up without bending and stooping.

This was followed by another six-month waiting period. Then we began discussing the next step: the final embellishments. After a long period of debating, I finally decided to go for one more surgery. On March 4, 2013, I had nipples made with a five inch chunk of skin taken from my stomach. That began another wait-and-watch period. Then on December 5, 2013, I followed my plastic surgeon into his little back room. There was a long tray of sterile instruments, all shiny and sharp, along one wall, and a long counter full of machines along the back wall. I crawled up onto his table and he did one last fat graft, taking some fat out of my right breast to lift it up, and using the fat to fill a dent in my stomach. As he did this, he told me that he'd never put fat into a stomach before. Then he shaved my left nipple to make it closer in size to the right.

He did both of these procedures with local anesthesia. I honestly did not feel any pain. However, that was a horrifically uncomfortable procedure. I don't think you ever want to know what a fat graft actually entails.

Around this time, I began praying that God would show us both (myself and my plastic surgeon) when it was time to stop this long process.

If I had known at the beginning what a lengthy, confusingly painful journey this would be, I would never have chosen to do reconstruction. I'm so glad I didn't know, because I still think I made the right choice.

On Wednesday, January 15, 2014, I went to a follow-up appointment with my plastic surgeon. I went to the appointment, prepared to tell him that I had decided to try something new. It had hit me (again) that every surgery, procedure, and stitch was done to make me *look* normal. But I wanted to *be*

70

normal. I wanted to be just another woman out there – without the scars, discolorations, radiation tattoos, and cancer reminders. Somehow, every time I headed in to surgery, I expected this to be The One. And every time, it wasn't.

No matter how hard he works, my plastic surgeon can't give me what I had to let go of. I almost wrote "what cancer took from me." But I didn't. Because it didn't. Cancer didn't take my breasts. I surrendered them. Because I wanted to live – and that was a small price to pay for survival.

So I realized again that I will never be normal. But I can be me.

I began exploring other options and discovered mastectomy tattoos. There are many, many women out there who have walked where I'm stumbling along, and they've created their own normal. They've found a new beauty. They've created a canvas that tells their story with joy – replacing what they let go of with something they can hold on to with pride.

So I went in to that appointment planning to tell my surgeon that I wanted to stop reconstruction efforts and get another tattoo.

He came in, sat down in a chair facing me, and slowly said that he was sorry. He couldn't help me anymore. He said he felt like we'd been running a marathon, and we could actually see the finish line, but that he just couldn't get me there. He's not fully happy with the results, but there's nothing else he can do. At least, not now. Maybe someday in the future.

He loved the idea of a mastectomy tattoo.

As I sat there, listening to him talking while slowly nodding my head, I was thinking, "Okay. He wants to stop. That's what I wanted, too. So why am I suddenly trying not to cry?" And I realized that he was giving up. The doctor who, from day one, had kept saying, "Yup. We can do that," was suddenly and abruptly admitting defeat. "I'll see you in a year."

After three years of seeing him every three months or more, six surgeries and a handful of procedures, and who knows how many stitches, he gave me a hug and walked me to the door.

For a moment, it felt like cancer had won. I was angry for a moment, too. How dare he give up on me! He promised! I was frustrated. I was scared. I was sad – I hadn't expected to say goodbye to him. It's funny how we can get used to seeing doctors, and actually start to miss them a little.

Then I was simply tired.

It had been a long journey. I'd been on this detour for almost seven years. But when I got home that day, I remembered the phrase that Abba whispered to me as I lay in my first MRI tube. "Be still, and know that I am God."

He is God. And not only is He God, but He is Love. And He is All Knowing and All Powerful. He answered my prayer and brought my surgeon and me to the same decision on the same day. He will never walk away from me, and He will never, ever give up on me.

18 HE HEARS

Sometimes I still weep. Sob. Curl up on the shower floor, rock, and wish. Sometimes I still cry on the way to work in the morning. I almost never see it coming.

I remember one ordinary Saturday morning. I slept until 7:00, got up, took my acid pill, played on the computer until I could eat something, had a snack, read a good book while I did six miles on the exercise bike, ate another snack while I cooled down and visited with my son. Then I went up to take a shower.

In the shower, as I washed my hair, my mind began to wander. It was about a month after the surgery to remove the expanders and put in the implants. This was supposed to be the last surgery on my journey. Unfortunately, there was a distinct lack of symmetry in size and placement. When I questioned him, the plastic surgeon merely smiled and repeated, "Just wait." In six months, all of the swelling would have gone down and then we could discuss the next step.

As my mind wandered, I began comparing the pros and cons of wearing the prostheses, and of the reconstruction I'd just gone through: daily discomfort or unconcealable deformity? Then I began plotting out my next discussion with my doctor. What can we do to fix this? I only wanted –

And suddenly I was on the floor of the shower sobbing. What had I wanted? I think, way deep down, I may have wanted this step to simply make all the other ones go away.

At my previous appointment, the nurse and I had talked about follow-up appointments. She decided that when I came back in three weeks they'd give me a referral for a surgical oncologist who can keep an eye on my cancer and make sure I get all the testing I need.

Encouraged, and again hopeful, I had headed back to my car. But as soon as I closed the door and turned on the engine, panic hit. *'Surgical oncologist'. 'Just to make sure.'* It was the kind of panic that comes suddenly from nowhere and makes it an effort to inhale. I fought for a few deep breaths, and whispered up, "Abba –"

Nothing else. There were no other words. Thankfully, He doesn't need words. He knows my head, and He holds my heart. The moment passed and life went on.

Until that Saturday when I stepped into the shower and the walls came tumbling down.

I had cancer.

I lost my hair.

I lost my breasts.

But I held on to my faith.

And I held on to my hope – maybe too tightly. I think I'd been hoping that this last surgery would just make everything right again. If it gave me back my breasts, surely it could give me back everything else.

But only God can do that. And, sadly, I think some things can be lost forever. Or, at least, for the duration of this life span.

So, even though I'm a very joyful person who's got a lot to be thankful for, sometimes I still cry. Even though I have access to such grace, sometimes I still wish longingly. Even though I have such hope, sometimes I still question. Even though I know He holds all the pieces of my beautiful life, sometimes I still worry and wonder.

The shrill part of my brain screams out, "How can you not be content? You're alive." The broken part of my heart whispers back, "But at what cost?" And the whole of me curls up, sobbing, in the loving arms of the Father. Knowing that the world is still turning. Trusting that this moment, too, shall pass. Believing that God is still in control and that all will One Day be well.

It often seems that my best praying is done in the shower. I collapse on the floor of the tub with the warm water rushing over me, sometimes mingling with salty tears as I pour out my hopes and fears for the day ahead.

My most heartfelt prayers are the simple one-word shouts inside my head at desperate moments. Help! Please! Why? How? Where?

74

God always hears me, and He always answers – just not always how I expect. Sometimes I don't see the answer right away.

One late lonely hospital night I silently screamed into my pillow "Grace! Grace! Grace! You promised me grace!" Over and over again. Two mornings later, as I was being discharged, a doctor put his hand on my shoulder and said that if he is ever faced with an illness like mine, "I hope I handle it with the grace that you have."

One of the things that cancer taught me was my constant need for God. Every moment is better when I bring Him into it with me. Now I find myself talking to Him while scrubbing the floor or walking around my house – just as I used to in the MRI tube and on the radiation table – and it brings a smile into my heart.

Pray without ceasing. That doesn't mean that I have to be on my knees all day. It simply means that I'm staying in touch with Him. I'm keeping Him updated on what's really going on, and I'm listening to His replies.

My Abba hears my every prayer. The long ones on my knees. The short ones in the shower. The whispered ones on the way to work. And the desperate one-word ones. He hears them all.

19 INSURANCE

There's a law I learned about on my journey: the Women's Health and Cancer Rights Act of 1998. According to this law, if your insurance covers a mastectomy, they must also cover reconstructive surgery and other mastectomy-related issues. Another law, the Health Insurance Portability and Accountability Act of 1996 (HIPAA) will keep a new insurance plan from declaring my cancer a preexisting condition. Because of these laws, every reconstructive surgery I have is fully covered by my insurance, as well as every prosthesis, every compression sleeve, and every mastectomy product. If I decide I want to go flat again, or go bigger, or change the size or profile of the implants, it will be covered by my insurance. Of course, that doesn't mean it's covered without a struggle, and without a deductible.

When I first received my diagnosis, we were facing budget cuts at work, and as a third-year teacher I was near the top of the list for being let go. If this happened, I would lose my health insurance. I did a little research on my options, neither of which was wonderful. I could buy into the COBRA plan for a small fortune or I could get unemployment insurance. The unemployment insurance would be cheaper but would offer fewer treatment options. Fortunately, neither was necessary. The budget was approved and we survived the year's end without too many cuts to the teaching staff.

This left me grateful to have insurance. I survived my cancer journey debt free. Not all survivors are that lucky. Not all survivors have insurance to begin with, and not all insurance plans have such small co-pays with zero deductibles. I was fortunate. However, I still became very frustrated at some of the hoops I had to jump through to get things covered.

During radiation, my left arm and hand painfully swelled up as my body made more and more lymph fluid to counteract the damage the radiation was causing. Because lymph nodes were removed during the mastectomy, this fluid built up in my arm as my body slowly created new channels for it to travel. I was diagnosed with lymphedema and given a compression sleeve and gauntlet to help push the fluid back out of my arm.

Shortly after I received the sleeve, a letter arrived from my insurance company explaining that lymphedema and compression garments were not covered by my policy. Because I really didn't like wearing the sleeve, I was a bit unwilling to pay the bill (which was the equivalent of two tanks of gas, a new pink Johnny, or a small Edible Arrangement bouquet).

When I called my insurance company to ask about it, the representative on the other end of the line patiently explained that compression sleeves are excluded by my insurance company.

At that point, I asked for clarification on what was covered after a mastectomy.

"Everything," he answered.

"Except compression sleeves," I added.

After a moment of silence, he admitted that though compression sleeves are excluded, the mastectomy negates that. They paid the bill.

My first tendency when receiving a bill was simply to stick it in my "bill box" and then either forget about it or simply misplace the box. That usually didn't help too much. Over the course of my cancer detour, I learned to pray about the bills I received in the mail, and then to call my insurance representative and ask questions about them.

Oftentimes the insurance company was on my side.

When I was admitted to the Berkshire Medical Center after my first chemo, there was a miscommunication between doctors, and I ended up being kept an extra day. I think they accidently forgot about me in my private little room with a great view of the fireworks (it *was* Sunday on the Fourth of July weekend).

Before he left on Saturday, my doctor popped in and promised me that if my fever stayed down during the night and my white blood cell count came up I could leave in the morning. However, he forgot to pass this information on to the nurses. My head nurse spent the day paging the doctor on call to discharge me, but he never got around to returning the call or stopping in to see me. I was told that I could discharge myself, but I wasn't sure what kind of effect this would have with my insurance company. Now I know that it would have been the best thing to do.

My parents had driven up to bring me home, and they hung out with me for the day. Finally, around 6:00 they gave up and headed home, leaving me behind for one more night. The head nurse spoke to human resources, and the head of human resources apologized sincerely for the misunderstanding as he handed me a couple of gas cards to reimburse my parents for the extra trip (an hour and a half each way). I was discharged first thing on Monday morning.

Then I received the bill. The hospital had submitted the request for reimbursement to my insurance company who had reviewed the request and paid for everything except that last night which wasn't deemed "medically necessary." I got the bill for the difference.

My poor bill box was over stuffed with "last notices" and collection agency threats before I finally decided to call my insurance company about it. My insurance rep was shocked that I had gotten the bill in the first place. She immediately called up the hospital and the debt was erased.

Another bill that came in was from an anesthesiologist. He wanted $900 for keeping me sedated during my mastectomies. I fully agree that he deserved every penny; however, I didn't have that much spare change lying around. This time I only waited about a month before calling my insurance rep to ask about it.

She explained that the hospital and the insurance company have a contract with discounted prices all listed out and agreed upon ahead of time. My insurance company had met their commitment. I was being billed for the difference between the agreed-upon discounted price and the actual cost of the procedure.

Part of the issue was that I had chosen to have my surgery in Boston and the hospital my surgeon worked with was out of network. However, after talking with me, the insurance rep decided that as I had been admitted into the hospital, I really didn't have much choice over who my anesthesiologist was. She agreed to pay the bill.

In February, I received a bill for radiation ($1200). Insurance took care of that one, too. Another bill they agreed to pay was for my prostheses and their holders (aka: breasts and bras). That was for $914. I called them the day the bill came in the mail and asked why it wasn't covered. She accessed my file and told me that the note attached said that I didn't get an authorization code first. I told her that I'd never heard about needing an authorization code, and she calmly explained that this was because I didn't really need one. She then sent the bill back to the adjuster for a review.

In April 2010, my employer switched to a new insurance carrier. Under my new policy, unless I am diagnosed with a new cancer, Dana Farber is no longer covered. However, once a year I give them a call and request special permission to visit with the oncologist who helped save my life. So far, each year, they've approved me for one more visit. I guess that's all I really need. One more visit. One more chance to sit and chat about old times before again hearing the word "remission." One more reminder that I've done well. That I'm doing well. That I'm going to continue to do well. That everything is going to be okay.

Which it is, because in all reality, I've got the Greatest Insurance Policy. I'm in Good hands. I'm in His hands.

20 SURVIVAL BENEFIT

Survival benefit.

That's a phrase I never used before cancer. And yet, it applies throughout all of life. There's a survival benefit in looking both ways before you cross the street. I feel very strongly that there's a survival benefit in wearing a helmet when riding a bicycle. I think there's a survival benefit in laughing, and I hope there's a survival benefit in eating chocolate.

I'm discovering that there's also a survival benefit in having good friends, and in asking them for help. And I've become desperately aware of the overwhelming, long-term survival benefit of leaning on Jesus.

He was the One with me on the bone scan tables and in the MRI tubes. He was the only One allowed in the locked bathroom on those long sick nights after chemo. He was the One Who was holding my hand when I woke up in the middle of the night realizing – *I have cancer!* He sat with me through those long lonely nights after surgery. He's the One Who understood all my skin aches and muscle pains from chemicals and shots – He's felt such pains from whips, thorns, and nails. He knows how it feels to have your body betray you. To be too tired to take the next step. His once strong body stumbled on the way to the cross.

The cross. The ultimate survival benefit.

When Christ died on that cross, His flowing blood met all the demands of justice. Our debts – every single one – were cancelled. And we *all* became survivors.

The shame is that so many of us are still living under our death sentence, when all we have to do is grab the wanted poster off the wall and throw it away. All we need is the courage and the faith to believe that, when Christ was crucified on the cross two thousand years ago, it was part of a plan. He agreed to do that. For us.

Because that was the only cure. That was how much He loved us.

Loves us.

Because He too survived. Risen from the dead three days later. That is my hope. Death is scary, but it is not the end. Pain and nausea are awful, but I am not alone. My cancer is big, but my God is bigger. This is just a detour in the road.

21 MY GOOSE

My cancer came at an awkward time for my son, although I suppose there never really is a good time to realize that your mother is mortal. I was diagnosed two months before his thirteenth birthday. I was weak, bald, and nauseous at the family cookout where we ate cake and ice cream for all of the July birthdays. He never even had his own party.

At a time when kids are normally self-focused and finding themselves, he was watching me and wondering if he was losing me.

I tried to be positive and honest with him every step of the way. I told him what I knew. I told him what the doctors said. I told him God was the One Who was really in charge. I brought him to my first chemo so that he could meet my doctor and see my infusion chair. I bought books on telling children about cancer, and I promised not to keep anything a secret from him, although I never overloaded him with details. I'd tell him when I had a test or screening coming up, and I'd tell him when the results came in. Then I'd simply be available to answer his questions as they came up.

One of the earliest tests I had done was the BRAC1 gene test. This test looked to see if I had inherited a mutated gene that could have caused my breast cancer. If the test came back positive the oncologists would lean toward a bilateral mastectomy and removal of my ovaries. It would also mean that my son, niece, and nephew could have the mutated gene as well.
We received the results while still on vacation in the Berkshires. I took the call while sitting in a folding chair on the porch. It was negative. I didn't have the mutated gene.

I hurried over to the fire pit where Wesley was sitting on the bleachers waiting for an archery class to begin and I told him the good news.

"What does that mean?" he asked me.

What does it mean? It means my cancer's not inherited. It means we don't know why I got it. It means I'm not high risk for another cancer. There are so many things that negative results mean, but as I searched for a simple explanation, an unexpected one popped out of my mouth.

"It means you won't get it."

Watching him respond to that was like watching a balloon deflate. He just relaxed, smiled, and went on with his life.

A few of the books I read about children and cancer say that the two things kids worry about most when their parents have cancer are that it's somehow their fault and that somehow they'll get it too. With our strong faith that God is in complete control, I don't think Wesley ever worried that any of this was his fault, but watching him respond to the results of the gene test made me realize that he may have been a bit worried about getting a diagnosis of his own.

My grandmother is a three-time cancer survivor. My father and my grandfather both survived prostate cancer. I had great footsteps to follow in when I began my own cancer journey. But although my son saw all of that, he had also watched his paternal grandmother take a much different cancer journey. Her cancer had metastasized to her brain. Wesley had faithfully visited her every other week, watching her lose the battle but win the war. She's Home now.

For Wesley, cancer had the potential to be very, very scary.

A third worry that children of cancer survivors often have is about what will happen to them. Who will take care of them if the parent becomes too sick to do so? How drastically will their daily life change?

I'm so grateful that my parents stayed with us throughout my cancer treatments. Mom drove me back and forth from the hospital, and Dad stayed with Wesley. Although life changed, there was still a safe stability in it. This was something I had worried about a lot. My parents were missionaries who would be home for months at a time, and then leave for years. This could be a bit tough on a little boy. It's also tough to live in two homes, and bounce back and forth between two parents. It didn't help that Wesley's father moved around a lot, too. I was the stability in Wesley's life. For me, the worst thing about cancer was the fear of not being able to be there when my goose needed me.

But God stepped in. And God clearly reminded me that He is the only true stability in this world. He promised me that He would never leave or forsake my little one, because He loves Wesley more than even my overprotective mother's heart can fathom. I don't ever have to worry, and neither does Wesley. There's a lot of peace in that. Of course, it also helps that Wesley is not quite as dramatic as I am.

Early on in my cancer treatment, I made the comment to Wesley that sometimes I really wish I didn't have cancer. His response was that it really hadn't changed anything.

I rebutted that it had stolen all my Thursdays. He pointed out that my Thursdays weren't that great anyway. I used to have to go to work. Now I didn't.

Then I asked if he'd looked at my head lately. He told me that it's not like I walk around holding a mirror. "But I can feel a draft." I whined.

"Wear a hat." He obviously adjusted better to change than I did.

Finishing up the treatments was like slowly waking up from a deep sleep. One day I remember feeling ready to be a mom again – but Wesley hadn't leaned on me in two years. He'd grown up while I'd been fighting for my life. I felt like I'd lost two years of his life. We had both changed so much, and neither of us could ever go back. We had to forge a new mother/son relationship. It wasn't always easy. He had to accept that I was back again and that what I said was final. I had to accept that he was a young man, ready to make his own choices and learn from his own mistakes.

During that vacation in the Berkshires when I ended up in the hospital for five days, my mom stayed with me in the hospital while my dad stayed at the camp with Wesley so he could finish up his vacation. At one point, my dad had asked Wes if he wanted to come up and see me in the hospital. Wes said no. But then he turned to my dad and asked, "Is it a good hospital?" My dad assured him that it was, and my son was comforted. He finished that week of vacation, then went back home with a friend.

And life went on.

It always has a way of doing that, doesn't it?

Surgeries, chemo, radiation – no matter what my oncologists threw at me, life went on. At one point, my radiation oncologist turned to me and told me that I was doing very well. "I'm trying to," I answered lightly.

"No," he told me seriously. "Considering everything we're doing to you, you're doing very well." Wesley did very well, too.

Eventually we got to the stage where everyone could take a deep breath and sigh in relief. We think we got it all, and we don't think it's coming back.

I'm part of a Young Women with Breast Cancer Study (of women who were diagnosed under 40) that researchers at Dana Farber are conducting. They took a piece of my cancer and some blood, and every six months I fill out a questionnaire for them. One time, I was filling out the questionnaire, and one of the questions was "How fearful are you about having a recurrence?" The choices ran from "extremely" to "not at all." I chose "a little bit." I am a bit concerned, because I really don't want to do any of this again.

The next question was "How fearful are your family members about a recurrence?" As Wesley was the only family member in the room at the time, I asked him. "I don't care," was his response.

Of course, I needed some clarification. I had him take out his ear buds and then asked him if that was an I-don't-care-if-you-get-cancer-again-and-die or an 'I'm-not-worried-I-know-we'll-be-fine.' So he explained. "It's okay if you get cancer again, because it really hasn't impacted your life."

My first thought was that he has been living on a different planet than I have. My life had been plenty impacted by this cancer thing. But my second thought was the peaceful realization that it hasn't impacted *his* life.

All this time, I've been worrying about what having a mom with cancer can do to a thirteen-year-old boy. And now I'm reminded – yet again – that it's all in God's hands. *We're* all in God's hands.

As a family, we'd tested God and He'd proven Good.

We'd leaned on Him and He'd proven Solid and Dependable.

We'd tried Him, and He'd proven Loving and Faithful.

God is good, and my goose is good, too.

I love those moments when I begin to worry and Wesley just looks at me patiently and reminds me again that God is in control. I laugh at the moments when he throws a snowball at an icicle that falls and shatters a sliding glass door. I thank God for the moments when I see him open doors for strangers, spend two weeks being homeless just to see life through someone else's eyes, and talk about his future plans.

His future is wide open. And it's in God's hands.

22 ROMANCE AFTER CANCER?

Most of the stories I've read of breast cancer survivors were about married women who talked about how kind and supportive their husbands were throughout the whole process.

But we don't all have that story. Some cancer survivors are too old to even want to go through treatments, sometimes they're too young to understand, and sometimes cancer sneaks into the single homes.

Family and friends gather around and welcome you into their homes where you are comforted and cared for, surrounded by unbelievable and unexpected love. But then the treatments come to an end, everyone goes home, and you're alone.

I don't want to be alone. I'd much prefer to walk with someone by my side, holding my hand, sharing the tough decisions and the ice-cream cakes of celebration. I want someone to laugh with, spar with, cry and pray with. To simply be beside.

But even if I found my prince charming today and had my fairy tale wedding tomorrow, what would stop him from having a heart attack the day after? A morbid thought, I know. But a simple reminder that God alone is in control. If I am going to demand control of one aspect of my life, I had better be prepared to control them all.

God alone can stop or start my cancer cells from growing. God alone knows which day His Son will return, and which day I'll be escorted into eternity. He knows what is scheduled to happen tomorrow, and who is standing around each corner. I've got a head and a heart full of hopes and dreams – things I want, things that I long for with my whole being – but God alone knows what is good.

There are just no guarantees that what we're daily striving to achieve will be what we're really wanting. If I'm not happy now, marriage, money, a cruise to Alaska won't make me happy. If you're not happy now _____ (insert your longing here) won't make you happy.

The trick is to ask God to step in and sift through the hopes and dreams in your heart. Let Him strengthen and grow the ones He's placed there and ask Him to remove the center beams of all the ones you've constructed on your own. Maybe my heart will feel like it's breaking as I watch my hopes crashing down around me. But it will be so worth it in the end.

Can you imagine the blessing and the joy that come with longing for what God Almighty longs for? Can you fathom the excitement that comes from knowing that God has the power and control to make it happen? The hope and certainty of God's kingdom on Earth.

No, I don't want to be alone. But I'd rather be alone than be outside of His glorious will for me.

There are a lot of worries that come with being a single cancer survivor: Will there ever be a man who can cherish me with the scars I've acquired? Who can love me, knowing my cancer might come back? Who will want to be a permanent part of this crazy roller coaster I didn't choose to ride? And how do you tell him that you don't have breasts? If you tell him too soon, will it scare him off? If you tell him too late will he feel like you've lied to him?

In my last dating relationship, my first since my diagnosis, I kept feeling like I had to apologize. A dear friend scolded me for that. "Don't you dare apologize for not having breasts!" she told me. A soldier coming home from the war wounded wouldn't have to apologize for losing his leg. I'd been through a war, and I'd survived. I had nothing to apologize for.

In the end it was the butterfly tattoo that broke the ice. He commented on it the first day we met, and I began to tell him my story. I didn't tell him all of the details on the first date, but eventually they came out. At the right time, in the right way. He handled it very well. Although our relationship ended, he gave me hope that a relationship after cancer was possible.

I thank God for that.

Solo or in sync. Alone or together. God's got a plan for our lives, and as He's proven over and over again, His plans are always good.

23 WALKING WITH ME

I didn't walk my cancer journey alone.

Yes, Abba was beside me the whole way. But there were also people walking with me. Coworkers, family members, friends. Caregivers. Granted, no one could walk the whole journey with me, but they took turns. I took very few steps alone. I once described my diagnosis as stepping onto a moving sidewalk. It wasn't necessarily moving too fast, but I had no control over the rate at which it moved, or the direction it went. No one was on that sidewalk with me, but everyone took turns grabbing my hand and running alongside me for a while.

My world wasn't the only one rocked by my cancer diagnosis.

It hit all of the people around me just as hard.

I was scared because I didn't know what would happen to me. They were scared because they didn't know what would happen to me, and what that would do to them.

We tend to wrap ourselves securely in the safe thought that the really bad things only happen to other people. But then it happened to me. When I received my diagnosis, everyone around me suddenly reeled back with the rock wall realization that sometimes the "other person" can be someone you know. Sometimes the other person can be *you*.

Each friend had a different way of coping with my cancer. Some just had to take a break from our friendship for a bit. Others took the opportunity to bring our friendship up a notch or two.

One dear friend became my Organizer of Joy. She took it upon herself to keep me smiling the whole way. She baked desserts and put them in my fridge. She wrote notes, taped them to gifts, and left them on my desk. She persuaded all of my coworkers to bombard me with hundreds of cards after my mastectomies and at key moments on my journey. She came to visit me after my surgeries, and drove me to appointments. One day she even called a radio station and had someone come visit me with tickets and a lollipop on National Smile Day. She just wanted me to know that I was loved – and she succeeded.

Another friend stayed up late making pink ribbon pins after I told her of my diagnosis. Then, after asking my permission, she quietly went to each of my coworkers, whispering the news and giving them a pin. She wanted me to know that they were behind me, rooting for me, there for me. After my surgery, she and another coworker spent hours knitting pink scarves. The day I returned to work, everyone in the building wore one to welcome me back.

My sister-in-law opened her house to me after rounds of chemo and surgeries. She tucked me into bed at night and got up to check on me. She made temptingly yummy snacks, and let me curl up with the dogs on her couch just doing nothing for a while. She also let me talk, and somehow always knew just what to say back. She understood cancer's bite and the fear that comes with it, because she had already walked on her mother's cancer journey and lived in the shadow of the one-day possibility of her own. Her mother lost that battle but won the war, and now dances headache free in the arms of our Savior.

Another friend became my surgery chauffer. She drove me to surgeries and appointments, and then waited beside me until I was wheeled in to the operating room. For the first couple of surgeries, she hung out and waited at the hospital, but then as we got used the whole routine she began to slip out and run errands. For one surgery, she went to work. When the doctor called to say I was in the recovery room, she headed back. They always said recovery would take about an hour; I think my average was three. After one surgery I slept in the recovery room for four hours. Then I'd slowly wake up and she'd drive me home, never complaining when I threw up in her car.

A dear friend at work became my prayer partner. She brought in lunch for me every Thursday and we'd eat, laugh, and pray together. My burdens always seemed lighter when I shared them with her. She also kept me well supplied with hypoallergenic soap and Free & Clear laundry detergent during the sensitive skin days of chemo and radiation.

A group of seniors at a nearby college were looking for a fundraiser to conduct. A friend mentioned my name and told my story. The girls decided to make beautiful crystal bracelets for breast cancer awareness and donate the proceeds to me.

When I heard about it, I asked if I could share the money with my neighbor who was now cancer free, but still paying for the treatments. The girls warned me that there would only be about $300 – but I told them that it was more about the emotional support than the actual money amount.

They ended up raising $500 from the bracelets, which they awarded to me at a Saturday night basketball game. All of the proceeds from the game were added in, too. During half time, I was called out onto the basketball court and presented with a check for $900, while the school mascot danced with my pink scarf.

Other friends visited, left cards on my desk, and baked apple pies and brownies. Some faithfully made meals for my son and me after every surgery. I think that was Wesley's favorite part. One day, after staring in the fridge for a couple of minutes, he turned to me and asked when I'd be having my next surgery.

My coworkers also created a sick day bank so they could donate their sick days to me if I ran out. Another friend came over and washed my hair after one surgery. Yet another friend stopped by to spend the day cleaning my house.

No, throughout this whole detour, I was never really alone.

So many times people would ask me, "How can I help?" I always found that a hard question to answer. Partly because I have a strong independent streak and hate to admit that I need help, and partly because while I was walking on my cancer journey I was often so befuddled that I really didn't know what I needed.

Now, looking back, I can see that what I needed was exactly what I got: the simple knowledge that I wasn't going through it alone. If you're a caregiver, a friend, a coworker, or simply an acquaintance of someone who's hurting and you want to know how to help them, just start by telling them you're there, and then just keep doing whatever you do. Place a card on their desk. When you make an apple pie for your family, wrap up a piece and give it to them. If your employer gives you free samples, pass some on to them. If you enjoy driving, offer them a ride. If you can push a vacuum, offer to do so in their living room. And when you see them, smile.

My son asked me who I was going to dedicate this book to. "I have no idea," was my reply. But as I thought about it, the answer became clear and simple. This book is for my caregivers. It's a thank you to everyone who helped me get this far. Thank you very much!

24 I DON'T LIKE MY CANCER, BUT I LOVE HOW GOD HAS USED IT.

I met a parent volunteer by the photocopier at school one day, and she told me that her husband had just been diagnosed with cancer. When they told their children, her second-grade son had turned to her and asked if it was "the hair kind," like with the teacher at school. She said that her children weren't scared because they'd seen me in the hallways and knew their dad would be okay. She thanked me.

One day when I was leaving a physical therapy appointment, my therapist suddenly told me that he really admired me for all I've gone through. I told him that he would do the same thing if he had to. He was quiet for a moment before he answered, "After watching you, I now have hope that I could."

Two years ago I had a high school volunteer who came into my classroom every morning to work with my little ones, and to learn how to teach. One day she sat down next to me and asked me about chemo. Her father was about to have his first round. We talked for a while about side effects and how she could help support him. She thanked me.

One day I received an e-mail from the parent of a former student. She doesn't have cancer, but she's at high risk and her doctor recommended prophylactic bilateral mastectomies and reconstruction. She just wanted someone to talk to. She wanted advice. She wanted details about that scary great unknown. We've e-mailed off and on ever since.

One October one of my coworkers was diagnosed with breast cancer. She popped into my classroom after school one day and asked all kinds of questions about finding good oncologists and how I chose to go to Dana Farber. She never said why, and I didn't ask. I waited. A week later she stopped by again and explained about her own diagnosis. Then she added that after having read my journals and traveled on my detour with me, she had hope that she could face this. And she has. Her joyfulness is an inspiration to all of us.

Twice Facebook friends have sent me messages just asking me to wait with them. They were faced with the horribly frightening possibility of a cancer of their own, and they didn't know how to tell the loved ones around them. So they whispered it to me. One of them joyfully thanked me when she shared her benign results.

I remember when my graduate professor found out that I had cancer. I started taking his calculus class shortly after I'd had my implants removed, a month after my mastectomies. I kept a hat over my almost bald head, and wore a bulky sweater to cover the drains still stitched into my armpits. It wasn't that first day but several classes later when the subject came up. I told him I'd be a bit late for the next class because my radiation appointment had been rescheduled. He looked at me, suddenly drawn and pale. "Cancer?" he whispered, barely audibly.

"Yes," I said with a confident smile. "But they got it out."

"Still, it's scary." He answered back. Then he talked for a bit about his wife and her cancer.

His words stayed with me for a long time. "Still, it's scary."

For some people, it really, truly is scary and horrifying. Cancer crashed in and stole someone they loved more than their own life – a mother, a wife, a husband. It destroyed their peace, shattered their hope, and left them fearful of the dreaded C word. I can understand that fear. I respect those people.

But then, there are other people who are afraid of cancer without any personal reason. It's just a scary word to them. It represents the great unknown. It reminds them of mortality and lack of control. I don't think it has to.

My grandmother is a three-time cancer survivor and I never even knew it until I received my own diagnosis. My grandfather was diagnosed with prostate cancer. I remember being scared when I found out, but he had the radioactive seeds implanted, and life went on as normal.

When my father was diagnosed with prostate cancer, I cried a lot. Not because he had cancer, but because I finally had to come to terms with the idea that my dad wasn't superman. He was human. He was mortal. It's tough to grow up, isn't it? My dad also had the radioactive seeds, and life went on.

So, when it was my turn, I figured that I would do whatever treatments my oncologist recommended, and that life would go on. Yes, there were very scary moments, but I didn't find "cancer" to be a very scary word. I want to share that. I want other people to have the added survival benefit of peace instead of fear if they ever hear the word "cancer" in their own lives.

The year after I was diagnosed I knew I'd be missing a lot of school days because of chemo, radiation, and surgeries. Also, I was still quite bald and refused to wear my wig. So I decided that instead of trying to hide it, I'd use it. I would teach my students what cancer is, how it affects us, and how we can affect it.

I found a coloring book about cancer and created a mini unit. Then I sent a letter home to parents explaining what I wanted to do and asking their permission. The response was amazing.

One mother wrote back and told me all about her sister. She had just completed her chemo and her hair was beginning to grow back. That student had just donated a foot of her hair to Locks for Love. She was already a pro on the subject.

Another mother wrote that her aunt was dying of metastasized cancer and they hadn't had the courage to tell their child yet. She just didn't know what words to use to explain cancer. She was so thankful that I was there to help her.

Other parents also shared stories, or thanked me for sharing mine. No one asked that their child be exempt from the unit.

I bought a book at Dana Farber called *Angels and Monsters*, a collection of pictures drawn by children with cancer. Each day we read a story about a child or teenager with cancer. Then we looked at the pictures they'd drawn and talked about their feelings and fears, hopes and laughter. The hardest part each day was turning to the last page of the book to see where that child was now. Because sometimes they weren't. Sometimes cancer wins. Sometimes cancer really is scary with a capital S. But my students would get so excited the times we saw a photograph of that little child all grown up and married with kids of their own. Because sometimes cancer doesn't win.

Like right now. My cancer didn't win.

Even if it were to crawl back into my body in this very instant. Even it were to glide into my bones or sneak maliciously into my brain and grow. Even if I were to give up my hope. Cancer has already lost. You just have to reread the beginning of this chapter to know that God has turned to good what cancer meant for evil.

25 HE LOVES ME

A couple of times during my cancer detour, I had the privilege to speak with a group of college students about my cancer and how God had been working through it in my life. The first time was with a women's group. It was a small gathering – fewer than twenty of us seated in a circle in a small room on campus. I spoke very briefly and then I let them ask questions.

One of the questions asked was if I ever got angry with God over my cancer. After a moment of quiet consideration I was able to say, "No." I had been scared. At times I was frustrated – mostly with myself and my new inabilities. I was also very, very sad at the changes in my life, and now and then I had gotten angry at cancer itself. But I was never angry at God.

At some points along the way, I did avoid God. And there were times when I didn't want to give Him control of my life because I was afraid of what He might choose to do. Things were okay, and I would cling to that instead of to Him. I still loved Him. I still worshipped Him. But the fear of having to do it all again just seemed to grow and grow until I would finally sit down and place it in God's hands again. And once, for just a moment in a second, I caught a glimpse of Who God is. Not just the Loving, Caring Comforter. But God Almighty. My Ruler. My Owner. I saw His Absolute Right versus my perceived rights.

God had a reason for each experience he brought before me. There was no wasted pain. And if He chooses to bring me through all of those experiences again, He has that Right.

And He'll have a Reason, because He loves me.

It's hard to be angry at the God Who's shifting around the pieces of the universe and orchestrating your life when you know beyond a shadow of a doubt that He's doing it all out of love.

The next question was, "How do you know God loves you?"

Again, I thoughtfully paused and pondered, but then a smile came across my face. How do I know He loves me? You mean, other than the everyday evidence He showers me with: sunrises, sunsets, kittens, laughter, children's soft handholds, and smiles. Then there are those extra-ordinary special moments when He reaches down and shapes my life in just such a way as to make me smile – because my smile in joy of Him triggers His smile in joy of me.

How many times has He shaped our lives and we haven't even opened our eyes to notice?

Oh, there are so many ways to answer the question of how I know He loves me. I know He loves me because the Bible tells me so. I know He loves me because He was willing to endure the ultimate torment of seeing my sin on His Son on that cross. He had to turn His back from His Own Son and endure the Greatest Separation, only to allow me to walk the streets of gold and be wrapped in His holy hands.

But those are all Sunday School answers that, while completely true, don't always satisfy the searching heart. How do I know beyond a shadow of a doubt that He loves me? I've tasted His love.

Even as a child, I remember craving love. My parents were good parents, but somehow we never fully communicated. I grew up feeling that I had to compete with God for their love and attention, and I knew I'd never win that competition. How could a little girl win against God Almighty? Finally, in high school, I cheated and declared the nonexistence of God. Surely if there was a god, life wouldn't be so painful. Such horrible things wouldn't be happening in the world around me. There wouldn't be war and cancer. There would be more love.

My senior year in high school, my graduating class of twenty-two students left the boarding school I attended to spend a few days up north. We stayed at a campground with mini golf and mountains. One day we all hopped on the bus and drove to a nearby waterfall to spend the day playing in the cascades. While my classmates hung out farther upstream, I perched myself on a rock toward the edge of the falls, letting the cool water wash over my feet. As I sat there I began to wonder.

What would happen if I simply slipped over the edge? I was so tired of the lonely search, of the questioning and the wondering. Of the longing that I didn't understand and I couldn't satisfy. Of wondering if I could be loved. I certainly didn't want to kill myself. I just didn't want to be.

But the pessimistic side of my brain pointed out that with my luck I'd fall down that waterfall, break every bone in my body, and live painfully ever after. The believing part of my brain worried that if God was real, He'd be plenty mad at me for giving up too soon. And the hopeful part of my brain just whispered, "Maybe…"

It was a long debate, but finally hope won out. I decided to wait. To enjoy the good days, to endure the long sad ones, to believe that love was possible, to stop living on the edge.

So I stood up, turned around, and started walking upstream to join my friends. But as I stepped forward my foot slipped, I fell and slammed my face on a rock.

I have a vague memory of a brief struggle. I was trying to move, trying to sit up, but someone was holding me down on the ground. Then I woke up.

If you had asked me my name I would have had no answer. If you'd asked me who or where I was, I would only have answered, "Loved!"

I was completely surrounded by Love. I was lying on my back, with my head in Love's lap. There were loving friends all around me – friends who cherished and loved me unconditionally. It was a place of ultimate safety. Ultimate security. Indescribable, unfathomable love for me.

I slowly regained awareness, first realizing that my hand hurt. Then throwing up a lot of water, and discovering that my head was throbbing. I slowly began to recognize some of my classmates around me and began to register their voices encouraging me to keep my eyes open and stay awake. The Love became less real, but it didn't fade or go away. It was still there. It's always been there. I just never noticed it before.

It turned out that I'd fallen down the waterfall. Some kind people at the bottom had fished me out. Then my friends came down and carried me back up to a deserted road where a missionary couple were just driving by in a truck with a clean mattress lying in the back.

They drove us to a friend's place. That friend then drove us back to the school. It was the weekend of the school committee meeting, so the doctor from the mission hospital up north was at the school. He met us at the dispensary. I wasn't very badly hurt – I had scratched the pad of my thumb and sliced both eyelids open, and may have broken a cheekbone or two. The doctor stuffed the fat back into my eyelids and stitched them up before sending me home. My best friend left the senior outing to rest by my side, holding my hand and helping soak my crusted eyes open again each morning.

I'd like to say that life was all happily-ever-after after that experience. But it rarely is. Our fairy tale ending comes later. I didn't change too much. For the longest while I still kept looking for love in all the odd places. And I still have problems – like cancer.

But I also have a very clear memory of a very special moment when a very real God opened my eyes and let me taste His love. I am cherished by the Creator of time. He stepped into time to show me that.

I clung to that all through my cancer. I never forgot that God loved me, though sometimes I forget how much He loves me. I forget about the love so great that it doesn't matter if I live or die as long as I can rest in that love. A love so real that simple transient things like pain or broken bones just can't compare. A love so strong that cancer and chemo just don't matter. Or, they do matter. They're just two of the circumstances I can joyfully endure to show my God how much I love Him back.

I don't remember what the rest of the questions were at that women's group. I don't know what message those other girls took home with them after that meeting, but I hope it got them thinking. I hope it got them questioning. I hope they went home, found a quiet spot, and asked their God, "Do You love me?" Because I know that's a question He never gets tired of answering.

26 GUILT TRIP

Not all stories have the same ending.

I remember the day we received the news that my uncle had passed away. His prostate cancer had spread to his bones. Mom and I still made our regular trek out to Dana Farber to receive my weekly dose of chemo. I think we talked about everything but cancer that day.

My next-door neighbor was diagnosed with breast cancer a couple of months before I was. I sat in her office, listening to her trying to process, trying to accept the shock of that invasion. She showed me all of the research she'd done on doctors and hospitals. She showed me her lab results, which she hadn't yet worked up the courage to read. I didn't know what to say, so I simply asked her if I could pray. She cried and we prayed. She had a lumpectomy. Then a mastectomy. Then moved on with her life.

It's easy to look around and see all of the people with different stories. Sometimes I wish… But God's asked me to live *this* life, not that one.

My paternal grandmother was a three-time cancer survivor. My son's paternal grandmother died of lung cancer that metastasized to her brain.
My coworker's husband and I started chemo at about the same time. While mine made me sick, his made him feel better for a while. But then I gained weight and he lost weight. I got better. He slipped away.

At his wake, all I could say was, "I'm sorry." Which meant so many things. "I'm sorry you don't have a husband anymore." "I'm sorry your daughters don't have a father." "I'm sorry my God chose to let this happen." "I'm sorry I'm standing here alive, and he's dead."

Survivor guilt is the feeling that you've done something wrong by surviving a traumatic event that others haven't – an earthquake, a lay-off, a war. It's also a common side effect of cancer.

I stood there at the wake between my coworker and her husband's casket, crying and feeling that something had just gone so horribly wrong. He'd worked in the before-school program and I remember looking for him each morning when I got to the building. I'd see his bald head in the cafeteria, and I'd know that it was a good day. I told my coworker that he was my inspiration, my hope that kept me coming to work.

But now he was gone. His cancer had won. And for the moment, I wasn't afraid of my cancer anymore. I was afraid that a mistake had been made, that the wrong person was in the casket.

How does one deal with that?

I guess we don't.

I guess this is just one of those times when God must be God and I must just be me. Why did my story get this ending? Why didn't his? Why didn't Uncle Marvin's? I wasn't loved more than them. I wasn't loved less than them. I wasn't more motivated. I wasn't better in any way. I didn't do anything special. I just survived.

Why?

At first, they all seem to be the same story: Once upon a time an ordinary person was living an ordinary life when all of a sudden cancer came along and made them extraordinary. And that's when the stories begin to differ.

Since my diagnosis, my student's aunt, two coworkers' husbands, my coworker's father, a student's father, my grandmother's nurse, my pastor, and my mother's brother all died from their cancers.

Yet mine shrank.

At surgery, 80% was no longer viable, and that we removed. Then I had more chemo and six-and-a-half weeks of radiation. I didn't die.

Some people survive a cancer diagnosis and go on to do incredible things to make the world better. Others simply survive and go on, which to those around them is an incredible thing that makes the world better. And then, there are those who don't survive.

I'm probably getting the quote wrong, but sometimes my Christian walk reminds me of the poem about that famous military charge: "Theirs not to wonder why. Theirs not to make reply. Theirs but to do and die." We just have to keep marching, even when our orders don't make sense. The comfort? Our orders aren't based on vanity or false information. Our orders come from the One Who created the world, and Who loved us all enough to let His Son die to bring us safely home.

That's where the survivor's guilt would make sense – innocent Jesus dying to save guilty me. And yet, when Jesus died (and rose again!) all guilt was banished. All guilt.

So I don't need to deal with this. He already has.

27 LEFT BEHIND

Death.

It's scary. For those of us resting in Abba's arms, it's just a doorway. Not only that, but it's a doorway through which we've caught glimpses of an awesome party happening, a party we know we'll be invited to someday.

But it's still scary.

My grandfather used to say that he wasn't scared of death. It was the dying part he was nervous about. But he did okay. He did well. He lay there, looking into Grammy's eyes, trying desperately to tell her that he loved her one last time. Then he was in Abba's arms, hearing God tell him how much He loves him for the first time.

Death means change. It means pain. It means the loss of everything comfortable and familiar. It means letting go and stepping into the unknown. Or, much, much worse, it means letting someone else go and standing here, on this side of the door, shut out of the party and alone.

It's even harder to be the one left behind.

My biggest fear when I faced my mortality wasn't my own death, but the impact that my death might have on my thirteen-year-old son. However, God, with His ability and wisdom to see around corners and know the past and the future, always knows best.

I put my son in God's hands the day He gave him to me in an eight-pound, eight-and-a-half-ounce package. And I gave him back to God the first day he went away with his father with a bag of diapers and his favorite pacifier. And again the day he first got on the bus to go to kindergarten. And the day he first got behind the wheel himself.

Once, years ago, I knelt down before bed to spend some time visiting with Abba. "Would you do what Abraham did?" He asked me. Would I sacrifice my son? I was startled and I answered without hesitation: "No way!" He asked again, and I again refused, listing off all of the reasons that this would be absolutely out of the question: it's illegal, he's my son, people would think I was mad, I'm a pacifist, it's simply too horrifying to think about. I love him.

I was on my knees for a long time that night as Abba and I wrestled back and forth – over my son. Finally, humbled and sobbing, I whispered, "Yes. If You asked, I would give You my son." Fortunately, He never asked. He didn't really ask for Isaac, either. He just wanted Abraham. He just wanted me to truly place Wesley in His hands.

So I did.

And I gave him back to God once again with my cancer diagnosis.

Wes makes jokes about "when" he'll get cancer.

The first time he did I snapped at him, saying he never would. He asked, "Why not?" He pointed out all of the family members who've had it. Then he firmly reminded me that God was in control.

I get upset when Wesley talks about getting cancer because I don't want him to ever face that. But I can't write his story. Even if I were all powerful and could orchestrate every event in his life, I'd never fully comprehend the ripple effect each of these events will have on the world around him. I don't have the knowledge or wisdom, or the inclination, to play God with my son's life. So I opened my fingers and let him go.

God *is* in control. My head knows that. My heart clings to that on the dark and lonely days. I really don't have to be scared. I shouldn't be scared. Though somehow I still am. But even then, He is faithful. He's always faithful. Even when I'm not, even when I'm afraid or doubting. Even when I'm turned around and running in the opposite direction. Even when I break my own promises, He always keeps His.

Even if my cancer comes back and whisks me though that doorway into that glorious party leaving my now nineteen-year-old son behind, God is faithful. Even if Wesley were to get cancer, and I were the one left behind. Because I won't be alone.

The one who rose from the dead to keep His promise to us walks beside me on my journey. And He is a faithful traveling companion.

28 PICKING UP THE PIECES

I had cancer.

I don't know why I had cancer, but I know there was a reason – because God screens my calls and he let this one through. God could have prevented me from getting cancer. But He didn't. God could even have healed me and made my cancer shrink without the chemo and surgery. But He didn't.

And I didn't ask Him to.

The deacons at my church asked if they could pray over me. I let them, but I felt a little uncomfortable about it. I was afraid that they would demand my healing and that God would answer their prayers simply because He loved them. But I didn't want to live with answered prayers. I wanted to live within God's will. Whatever that was.

So I didn't pray to be healed, but I did pray and I was healed. After four rounds of Adriamycin and Cytoxan, four biopsies, fifteen surgeries, six-and-a-half weeks of radiation, four doses of Taxol, eight of Abraxane, and thirty-four of Herceptin, I now say I am cancer free. The surgeon says I'm in remission, but that because it's been six years since the cancer was removed, I can breathe a sigh of relief. My medical oncologist has told me that there's little chance of recurrence. It's time to move on with my life.

But how *does* one pick up the pieces and go on the day after a catastrophe? I suppose we do it the same way we start off every day. We wake up. We get out of bed. We step forward.

Thinking about rebuilding a whole life shaken to its foundation is scary and overwhelming, but thinking about enjoying today, taking a class, buying groceries for the week – those things are doable.

Last May, I adopted a cat. She's a gorgeous diva with black fur and a white star on her belly. She gets me up bright and early every morning and keeps me company every night. She runs around the house chasing flies and headbands and steals anything soft. She was three and a half when I adopted her and she had already had at least two homes before coming to live with me. Her last family gave her up because she "needed too much attention." After that, she spent three months in a cage in a shelter. Although she's only been with me a year, it feels like she's been a part of my life forever.

For the longest time, I was afraid to get a pet. The what-if's just loomed too large. I couldn't make a commitment like that – what if I got sick again? What if I needed another surgery? What if I grew too tired? How do you tell a cat that you're dying?

Cancer can take away your ability to make long term plans and commitments.

But God can give it back.

When I first got Stella, she was very skittish. Soon, she worked up the courage to explore. She would roam around the house, but every now and then she needed some reassurance. She'd crouch down and begin crying and wouldn't stop unless I was touching her. At those times, I sat down on the floor next to her and just rubbed her head with both hands, keeping up a steady stream of gentle one-sided conversation.

"I love you, Stella. I'm right here, because I love you. I'll go away for a couple of hours, but then I'll come back, because I love you. You'll be fine. You can go explore, and I'll still be here. Because I love you."

Though she was comforted by my hands and my tone, I don't think she understood my words. But as I kept up the reassuring whispers, I realized how familiar they sounded. That's what my Abba is whispering down to me in my total panic moments. He will always be with me – because He loves me.

My future isn't written yet, though God holds it in His hands. Right now it's a blank page with a million possibilities, and I find that very, very exciting.

I've got to find a new normal now, by moving forward.

In my new life, normal is the sound of raindrops outside my window. Normal is a day I don't feel like throwing up, or a night I sleep through. Normal is asking for and accepting help graciously. Normal is laughing out loud. Normal is getting most of the bills paid on time, and wearing a pretty shirt to work. Normal is exercising every day that I have the strength and the inclination, swinging on my porch swing, playing games on the computer, and reading a good book. Normal is finishing a project for a class, and grading a pile of papers. Eating a bowl of ice cream just because I want to. Normal is doing dishes, doing laundry, or sitting on the couch doing absolutely nothing. Normal is waiting. Normal is holding on to God's promises, God's grace, God's love. Normal is letting Him be in control.

I can never go back. So I'm going to move forward.

I'm going to love every moment that I can and simply endure the rest. Wasting none, growing through all, and always loving God. I'll take an allergy pill and then smell the flowers, and I'll keep my eyes wide open.

I can do this.

Sorry. *We* can do this.

I'll pick up the pieces that are left and I'll let God rebuild me a new life shaped by what I've been through and what I've learned.

So what have I learned?

Well, one thing I've learned is that death doesn't have to be scary.

It's simply a transition. I know exactly what happens next. To be absent from the body is to be present with the Lord. During my journey, I read many books about people so afraid of dying, people so desperate to live for just one more day, who'd have done anything – regardless of quality of life – just not to die.

I *was* afraid – of the unknown, of what could happen, of the possibility of pain. Sometimes I became frozen in fear. There are cold, dark places that sunshine can't reach. There's a knot that wedges itself between my throat and my lungs and each breath has to struggle to get past it. Sometimes I'm afraid to step forward because I have no idea what is lurking around the next corner. If I can get cancer, if I can lose my breasts, anything can happen. There is nothing safe, and I get scared.

But I don't need to be afraid of dying. When it really is my turn to go Home, my Abba will meet me at the door. I'm ready. Are you?

29 CELEMOURN

The first anniversary of my diagnosis day was a tough one. My best friend had to put her dog down that day. I sat with both of them in the grass outside the veterinarian's office as they injected the chemicals that made her drowsy and then stopped her heart. I stood beside my friend as her husband laid their cherished one in the ground and covered her with a blanket of dirt.

Then we both got tattoos. To remember.

We chose to get matching butterflies, mine on my chest with the antenna wrapping around a radiation dot. Hers is on her foot. Over the years, I've gotten so many comments on that butterfly tattoo. Each time it makes me smile, and it gives me hope. Sometimes I just say thank you and move on, but often I tell them what it means and why it's there, and how good my God has been to me.

On my second diagnosis day I began making plans to get new breasts.
On my third diagnosis day, I got tat two. It was the tat man's day off, but he was willing to come to work anyway when I explained why. I showed him the scar down my back from reconstruction, and then picked out a flowering vine from the posters on the wall. His wife dug through her book of patterns and held it up against my scar. It was a perfect fit. The vine wrapped over the scar, and a little curlicue came out to the side to wrap around a small drain scar.

There was a lot of nerve damage and scar tissue, so I had large pockets of numbness. At times I could only feel the weight of his hands and the vibration of the needle. Then as he was working, the needle would suddenly hit healthy skin and I could feel every single needle prick. As I sat in the black chair, contorting myself into the positions that would flatten the skin he was working on, I realized that I was actually enjoying the pain of the needle. It was a pain that I had chosen. A pain that I had complete control over. I could stop this process any time I wanted. It was a pain that was going to take ugliness and make it beautiful. I was taking back a bit of the ground that cancer had stolen from me, and it felt good.

My fourth diagnosis day was when I coined the term "celemourn," a combination of celebrate and mourn. It actually should be mournancel, but that just doesn't sound as good. I decided to begin the day by mourning, and by acknowledging all that I'd lost and given up on this cancer detour. By being upset and letting myself cry. Then, the plan was to slowly transition into a celebration of how far I've come, ending the day remembering that I had survived.

That morning, I decided to climb Mount Greylock and stand on the highest spot in Massachusetts. There's a tower on the top that you can climb and see the world from.

It was a foggy, misty day so instead of hiking, I drove to the top. When I got out of the car and looked around, I couldn't see the tower anywhere. I pulled on a jacket and a hat and began walking. It really didn't matter which direction – you couldn't see more than a yard in front of you. As I walked I realized that there is so much more to life than cancer, work, making supper, and doing laundry. Surviving is so much more than getting up each morning and going to bed each night. It's walking against the wind, laughing in the rain, and stepping blindly into the fog knowing that God will catch you when you fall – either in this life or the next.

I made a list of all the things I'd lost in the last four years: my breasts, my childlike views, my health and my breath, my five-year plans, my trust that all is good, my ability to laugh at life, my faith in a happy future, my lack of fear, my sense of immortality. But as I listed each item, a part of me shouted, "Not true!" My hair grew back. My new five-year plans are still good. I still trust God. I can still laugh. I was always afraid, even before I was diagnosed with cancer. And I've gained so much. He loves me. My future will be different than I'd planned. But it will still be beautiful. It will still be.

As I walked, the tower suddenly appeared out of the mist right in front of me. I opened the door, stepped inside, and climbed the spiral staircase. I don't know what I was expecting or hoping for, but there was no view from the windows at the top. They didn't even really seem to be windows. Because of the fog they were just gray panels letting in a tiny bit of light. But I found what I was looking for at the bottom of the stairs.

On the wall, inscribed over the door, was a quote: "Life is no life to them that dare not die." What's the point of living if I'm always going to be afraid of dying, just waiting for the cancer to return? If I'm always going to be afraid of my future, just because I can't see what's ahead, I'll miss out on the present. That's not life.

So I began to celebrate. I had new bumps. No, not breasts, but enough for now, and maybe someday I'll realize I don't need more. I had family and friends, and peace with myself – who I am and who I am becoming. The farther away I get from diagnosis, the more I realize how little I have to mourn and how much there is to celebrate.

On my fifth celemourn, I went for a walk with a pad of paper and worked on this book. The day before had I celebrated the previous five years with two of my friends. We'd gorged ourselves on ice cream and laughter as we spent two-and-a-half hours in a restaurant booth simply enjoying life.
I sat down to take inventory again. I tried to think, to dwell, to process. I even tried to cry, but the tears wouldn't come. Today was good. My heart was at peace.

I mean, really, what has cancer done to me?

It took away my little breasts, but I ended up with bigger bumps. Granted, I will never feel the touch of a hand on my breast again, and if I ever have another baby I won't be able to breastfeed. That's sad.

But it's not the end – of me, of hope, even of life as I know it.

My life is still so full of so many other pleasures. Sitting in the sun, walking beside the lake, listening to music that makes my heart dance, watching my son graduate from high school number three in his class, watching him race and take first place, finding the perfect shade of nail polish to match my mood, seeing the I-get-it! light click on in a second-grader's eyes, holding hands while walking through the park, laughing hilariously over a banana split with decadent chocolate ice cream and hot fudge, prayer time kneeling by my grandmother's chair, an unexpected e-mail from Africa, watching the butterflies visit the flowers in my Mother's Day garden.

I could fill this book with the blessings He's showered down on me.

Well, actually, I guess I already did.

For my sixth celemourn, after celebrating all of the five-year anniversaries, I planned to climb Mount Greylock again, this time with friends. We were going to reminisce on the way up, and laugh all the way down. That Friday night, as I prepared to crawl into bed after a long day of working and grading papers, I suddenly realized that I had somehow gotten the dates mixed up. I'd been thinking that my Diagnosis Day was the next day, but it had actually been that day. I'd forgotten all about it. It was just another day.

My seventh diagnosis day is only weeks away. The detour is over now and I'm merging back on to the main highway. I'm not scared anymore. I'm excited about all of the possibilities. I'm ready. It's time.

Yes, it's time.

I've had seven years. *And* I have today.

Let's celebrate.

30 THE FINAL CHAPTER

So what happens now?

Seven years after diagnosis, six-and-a-half years after the mastectomy, six years after the last round of chemotherapy and a temporary clean bill of health. What happens now?

I guess I just keep doing what I've always been doing.

Living life and praising God.

Yet there's always that whisper in the back of my mind: *What if it comes back?* There are still those moments when it suddenly hits me – *I had cancer!* And those times when I read a magazine article full of glaring statistics. "Eighty percent of women diagnosed with breast cancer live five years beyond diagnosis." And I glance at the busy world around me thinking, *I want so much more than five years!* So how do you keep on going through the motions of normal with all of this sitting on your heart?

And that's when God whispers down, "You're not going through any motions. *This* is normal now. And, yes, I am still in control."

I remember the end of seventh grade, when it was time for everyone to leave boarding school and go home for the summer. Some were going to Mali or Burkina Faso. I was going down to Abidjan. Other friends would be going off to other African countries, some back to the States. We would be scattered all over the globe. After living so closely with all of these friends, it was quite a frightening thought to be going home to a quiet house with only my parents and my brother.

I had one friend who lived in Bouake, the town the school was in. His parents weren't missionaries, which put him on the bottom of the enrollment list. Any missionary kids coming to the school had priority over him. So, he had no idea if he'd be coming back to school. Our goodbye might be forever.

But we knew that our God is forever, too.

He wrote a chorus in my scrapbook. "God holds the future," he promised me. "There's nothing to be afraid of."

How true that is. But sometimes, how hard it is to believe! It's a truth we need to dwell on constantly until our heart can hold on to it during the long dark nights.

When I came back to school my junior year, I'd changed a lot. I was less shy. I wasn't content to be in the background anymore. I wanted to stand out and be noticed. I constantly made jokes and tried to keep people laughing. Life was fun. But it was also sad at times. I missed my friends in the States. I missed my family.

One day I sat flipping through old yearbooks and photo albums, remembering, and I found that quote. I reread it, wondered if it were true, and I clung to it just in case.

Life *is* worth living. There is a point to it. And it's Him. Not me. Not happiness. Not laughter. Not clarity or simplicity. Not complete understanding. Simply Him. Simply because He's alive. I decided that was *my* song. But I'd still never heard the rest of it. I only knew the chorus.

Years later, when I went back to Cote D'Ivoire on a missions trip, I sat down to talk with my mom. We had a deeper talk than we'd ever had before. During our conversation, I told her about that chorus. "It's my song," I told her.

"Yes. It is," she answered with a smile.

Then she told me about when I was born, about her worries and her fears. She'd wondered what she was doing bringing a baby into such a war-filled world. All the crime, all the pain and financial struggles. She worried that she'd made a mistake. She worried for that baby's future.

And God answered all those worries.

On my first Sunday, she carried me into the sanctuary at Adam's Square Baptist Church just as the congregation began to sing the second verse to "Because He Lives" by Bill and Gloria Gaither – the verse that talks about holding a newborn baby, and knowing that that baby will be able to face all that life brings because Jesus lives. It was the same song I'd had written in my yearbook all this time. My mother was comforted with the calm assurance that I was in God's hands. That I could face the uncertain days ahead. And I did. And I still do. Because He lives. Whatever comes next, comes through Him.

A few years ago, on our annual vacation in the Berkshires, I went to a Christian coffee house. As I sat there eating chocolate cream puffs and mozzarella sticks, I suddenly realized that the band was playing my song. I stopped eating and listened, and it felt like God was speaking to my heart. I'd spent most of that vacation wrestling with how I'd pick up the pieces of my life, after cancer and treatment. I'd spent hours with God wondering what would come next, and here He was reminding me that I don't have to wrestle or wonder. I can claim that calm assurance that He promised me when I was an infant. These are the uncertain times He was talking about then. I can face them because He lives, because He allowed Himself to be nailed to a sinner's cross and wore my every crime and shame to death, leaving me sparkly clean and calmly assured, because He rose from the dead to show me the way to Life.

Today, I'm not very worried about how my story will go. I know how it will end. I'll leave this body, and the Holy Spirit Who has shared it with me will bring me before Jesus, Who will then bring me before God. God, seeing me between the Beloved Son and the Holy Spirit, will see me as His own child, and He'll wrap me in His arms and welcome me home.

That's how my story will end.

At the very beginning of eternity in God's arms.

ABOUT THE AUTHOR

Monica Nelson is an elementary teacher and seven-year cancer survivor currently living in Charlton, Massachusetts. A former missionary kid, she writes devotionals and praise poetry, as well as gently humorous essays about cancer treatments and their side effects. She also posts frequent anecdotes about Stella, her rescue cat, and Wesley, her nineteen year old son.
You can find her website at livingcancerfree.weebly.com.

Made in the USA
Charleston, SC
25 April 2014